Benito Santiago
Behind the Mask

My Life of Baseball

Benito Santiago
With
Charlie Hudson

(A: Ana Rivera)
*recuerdo de ser amiga que le
desea lo mejor junto a foma
gracias por seguir mi carrera)*

(Benito Santiago)

Table of Contents

Chapter One
An Unlikely Beginning

"I didn't want anyone to know I was shaking inside. The judge wasn't trying to scare me, but I was only eleven years old, and if I said the wrong thing, I thought she would make me leave the family I loved. I didn't know about my other family until I was ten, and I didn't want to live with them."

Benito Santiago has no memory of his father or the events surrounding a critical time when he was an infant. It is a story of perhaps destiny, yet also of the choice of a woman who could have walked away from a situation for which she had no responsibility. The tale of how Benito came to have two families was portioned into pieces, small bits explained over time as he grew older and could grasp the answers.

"I was born in Ponce, Puerto Rico, on March 9, 1965. We were rather poor. My father, Jose Manuel Santiago, drove one of the trucks carrying cargo from San Juan to Ponce. They called him 'El Capitan' because he always had a shipping captain's cap on. He was very handsome in his photographs. During his work, he would deliver loads of concrete to Modesto Gonzalez in Santa Isabel where he was building a house for his family. My father and Modesto became friends.

"The road between Ponce and San Juan was rather dangerous in those days. It was not like the wider roads now, and there were steep inclines with not much room for big vehicles. I was only three months old when the truck began to slide off the road and my father fell from the truck to free himself from the crash. He was injured, but like a lot of village people, he wouldn't go to the hospital. They preferred home remedies. When he finally went to the hospital, it was all bad news. He was quite ill and without much hope given to him from the doctors. It seems as if he knew he was not going to live for long. While he was there, Nelida Gonzalez, Modesto's wife, was in the hospital because one of their girls had broken her arm. She saw 'El Capitan' and in talking with him, he asked them to come to pick me up from where I was at my sister's and take me to their house to raise me. He told her I was very young and very weak and my mom already had five more children. I don't know why he felt it wasn't good for me to stay with the family I was born to, but it was his last wish that I be picked up from where I was and to be raised by Modesto and Nelida.

"After 'El Capitan' died, Nelida kept her promise. I don't know where my mom was at that time because I was later told my older sister took care of me. Nelida picked me up in the house where my sister had me and took me to their house. She had not told her husband, Modesto, about the promise, and he had known nothing about the death of his friend until he came home and saw a baby lying on his double bed. Nelida told him they had to keep the baby because she wanted to raise him. Modesto said he didn't want more babies in the house because they were too old and of their five children, Eneida, Nelson, Luis, Maria Luisa, and Evelyn, their youngest was already thirteen. He was tired and wanted to rest from having small children. When I was old enough to ask questions, Nelida told me about the wish of my father and that she said to Modesto, 'Look at this child's face. I want us to take care of him.' This is how they saved my life, and until I was ten years old, I called them Mom and Dad and they called me Papo."

Santa Isabel is on the southern coast of Puerto Rico, a town of eight districts where nearly half the population lives below the poverty line and the unemployment rate rarely drops below 15 percent. With modern highways, it takes approximately an hour-and-a-half to drive to San Juan. Prior to the current roads, though, it was not an easy trip to make. Benito recalls the boundaries of his childhood.

"In Santa Isabel where I grew up, we were between the mountains and the sea. It was an area of sugarcane fields. Our baseball field was surrounded by cane, and the train used to pass from one side to another sector around the field. We used to love riding on that train. The baseball, though, even at the young age, it was calling to me. When I was nine years old, I used to like hitting stones with a wooden stick to see where they went. One of them almost hit the teacher of the school, and I was forced to leave that game. Baseball was more than a game though. It was the way to have a dream. Mom and Dad worked hard, but the money was not enough to almost nothing. One day I asked my mom for fifty cents for something I wanted to buy and she told me she didn't have it to give me. I said, 'Mom, it's okay and don't worry. When I grow up and am a professional baseball player, I'll give you everything you need.' I don't know if she believed it was possible, but Roberto Clemente was a hero to every kid in Puerto Rico who touched a baseball. He was proof it could happen. There were other big league players, too, from Puerto Rico, but Clemente was who everyone always thought about first.

"Between the ages of ten and eleven were two important parts of my life. This was when I learned about the family I had in Ponce, a town only twenty miles away. My birth mother, Ivette Rivera Resto, came to our home and told my mom that it was time I came to live with her for now. I was to return to my place as the youngest with my brother and sisters, Irene, Magda, Jose, and Luisa. She said she had only allowed Nelida to take me because she was very sick and sad after the death of my father, 'El Capitan.' To me, Nelida was my mom, and even though I had grown considerably, she and Modesto had sacrificed their lives to keep me and raise me as God commands. They understood why my father had asked them to take me, and they did not want to surrender me to live in the environment where she (my birth mother) lived. You can imagine how confusing it was for me. A woman from the government came many times to visit. They didn't try to explain all that was going on, but she did spend months on the case. The whole thing was very ugly because I was underage and it was going to be up to the judge who was handling the case. My mom, Nelida, had cried a lot and told me, 'Papo, don't worry that you are going to go with them.' I didn't see how it would be right to make me leave.

"There must have been a lot of discussion about me, but what I remember was being afraid to say too much. What if I said something I didn't mean to and the judge didn't understand? I was scared of that, but it turned out the judge was very calm in talking to me. She asked me who I wanted to go and see—my mother who brought me into this world, or the family that taught me to live in this world and gave me love and understanding? I chose Modesto and Nelida, and for a long time after that, I had no contact with the family in Ponce. I have never regretted choosing Nelida and Modesto. Another piece of this I didn't know was when I was little, Jose Manuel Santiago, who was called 'Dog,' was always aware of me in town. I only thought he was an older kid and didn't find out he was my real brother until after the case was opened and we went to court. Jose Manuel got along very well with Modesto and Nelida, and he is still my real brother because of how we were born and how he was in my life understanding I was better off not being with my birth mother.

"The other part that was very important is I was playing baseball on a regular team with Angel Cruz as the coach. He's a very good teacher and player and stayed in Santa Isabel as the coach for decades. He saw I had a good throwing arm and I was a pitcher in the sixth grade and threw seven or so no-hitters. I competed all over Puerto Rico, but I was also a clean-up hitter. [A clean-up hitter is fourth hitter in the lineup and is traditionally one of the strongest batters.] I threw fastballs and curves and then I started playing shortstop as I got older and moved up into the next age category. Everyone wants to be a pitcher, and even though I was good, what I loved most was the position of shortstop. I threw some guys out in those first games I played as shortstop—maybe two or three—and my father was in the stands. Cruz was in charge of our team with Humberto Rivera, and they both put a lot of effort into me because they saw my talent early. You can love to play and work hard, but if the raw talent isn't there, it isn't.

"There were two baseball fields in Jauca where we played, the Tamarindo and the Destino. [Jauca is a district of Santa Isabel.] The first trophy I was given was tiny, five inches high, but I thought it was the most beautiful thing in the world. I slept with the trophy. It was later when I was a teenager that we had a game where the catcher couldn't play and we had to have a catcher for the game. Angel looked at me and said, 'Papo, you are going to be the catcher.' I didn't want to because I didn't think I was going to do well. I told him he was crazy, but Angel told me *I* was crazy. He said I had long fingers and convinced me to wear the catcher's gear for the first time. He was right, and I threw seven of nine players out who tried to make it to second base. I liked the feeling, and Angel said that it was easier to get to the big leagues as a catcher than as a shortstop and there would always be too many pitchers trying to make it. I told my father I wanted to be a catcher from then on, but that meant I needed extra equipment. We put money together to get me what I needed. My sisters helped by giving up money they had been saving for things they wanted. This is the kind of love we had in my family.

"Money is something we always had a hard time with. I started washing cars and could earn between two and three dollars a day, but the sad truth was if you wanted money, the way to get it was to be involved with drugs. The youngest kids would start simple with selling marijuana, and later other drugs. It was tough on the streets in Puerto Rico. A lot of my friends were caught in what seemed like this easy way to make money. Then they began to use drugs and ended up addicted and plunged into a life of crime with prison, or were killed by someone, or died from drugs. I had my talent as an athlete, and my parents taught me what was right and didn't want me to end up in the streets. As a teenager, you think you don't have to listen to your parents. My brother Nelson had a strong hand, and he stepped in to take care of and guide me, to try and keep me out of trouble. My best friend, who was like family, was rough and wise to the streets and didn't want me to be like him either. He and my brother weren't the only ones. There were other people in our neighborhood who seemed to understand that I had a real chance at baseball because of my talent. If I was hanging out where I shouldn't be, they would tell me to go home, go play ball, go away from the area where everyone knew trouble happened. Maybe I didn't listen as much as I should have, and for a while I did some things I wish I hadn't, but it didn't last for long. I wanted to play, and the more I became involved in baseball, the less time I had to be in the streets.

"In 1980, my friend Humberto Rivera was leading our team of Santa Isabel. We were one of the finalists of Puerto Rico, and we went to San Juan to play for the championship. One of the biggest scouts in baseball, Luis Rosa, was watching the games in San Juan and saw me play. We were practicing on a hot day with mosquitoes swarming around, but Mr. Rosa put on extra insect repellant and watched us the whole time. Mr. Rosa, who everyone knew as a famous scout, invited me to come onto his team of The Raiders in the American Legion in

San Juan. This was the first real step if you were going to have a chance at the dream of playing in the big league. The truth was I didn't like school and wouldn't study any more than I had to. If I was making D's and passing, that was okay with me. There wasn't any way for me to think of going to college and getting to baseball that way. Maybe I shouldn't have thought like that, but it was a common way of thinking for kids in Puerto Rico. When it came to baseball, I paid attention and was learning the game. To me, that was better than school would ever be, and I cared too much about baseball to listen to any advice about another career.

"Now with my time being divided between San Juan and Fajardo, school became even less important than before. My brothers Luis and Nelson Gonzalez had a car that was damaged, and it broke down a lot with us sitting next to it on the road to see if anyone would pick us up to give us a ride. Other times, we could make it to where we needed to go and someone else would take me home. Mr. Rosa did that a lot for me. In the times when we were waiting next to a broken-down car, my brothers would talk to me, give me advice, talk about how I could be something special if I would stay off the streets. I also remember what it was like when I was making those trips. Puerto Rico isn't a big island, but for me, the area where we lived was what I knew best. The mountains between Santa Isabel and Fajardo made a big impression on me. There wasn't a wide highway then, and I saw waterfalls, forests, and fields where famous fruits of Puerto Rico grow. The fertile land was very green, and in the times my brothers and I were broken down on the road, I would stare at it while we waited and talked.

"When we played games in Fajardo, Luis Rosa paid for the hotel, and that was something special. We slept in the Parador de Fajardo, a hostel near the docks where the boats left for the island of Vieques. Being on the water like that was very different than our neighborhood in Santa Isabel. What we did for lunch was parents prepared a big meal and after the game we ate in the park. We ate very well because the food was very rich.

"As good as my coach had been, I wasn't born with an instruction book for living new experiences and Luis Rosa helped me a lot in this. I was dreaming of the big leagues, but I knew I had to work really hard and gain strength in my arm to reach my goal. From the beginning of when I played, I did it to win. For me, that was what mattered, and I played 100 percent at each game. I was upset when we didn't win and would review the game in my mind to see what mistakes I made to learn from that and not make the same mistakes again. I was determined to do everything I could to win the next time. For me, this was learning, better than going to school because I wanted baseball to be my life.

"It was settled now. I would be a catcher, and when I watched baseball on TV, I saw Johnny Bench, Goose Gossage, Freddy Lynn, and Steve Carlton. I loved to watch how Gossage played, the way in which he threw the ball. When I was little, my favorite major league team was *La Maquinaria Roja*—the Cincinnati Reds. I also liked the New York Yankees and the Boston Red Sox, but Luis Rosa was scouting for the San Diego Padres at that time. If I was going to make my way in the minor leagues, that would be my path. It wasn't crazy for me to think this way because two players from Jauca reached the major leagues; Miguel Alicea was a Philadelphia Phillies pitcher, and Santos Torres Denis was an outfielder with Cincinnati. Sao Jose Guzman, who was right there from my town of Santa Isabel, signed with the Texas Rangers.

"As hard as I was working to prove I was ready for the big leagues, I met a girl, too, at a party one Saturday night. I had gone to eat at the Metropol in San Juan, which is one of my favorite restaurants in Puerto Rico. I met Blanca Ortiz, and at first, I didn't know how to talk to her, but I got to know her and we started dating. Blanca was from

Salinas; that's only ten minutes from Santa Isabel. We went to the movies, parties, and she came to the professional games in San Juan to see me play. We had a TV in the living room of the house in Santa Isabel. Every Saturday we watched the games of the big leagues, and we also used to go to a bar near the house in the neighborhood. We met many times to see the games, and I was in love with her.

"Age seventeen was a year I can never forget. I was going to make my old coach Angel, my family, my town, and other people in Puerto Rico proud. Luis Rosa had taught me what he could, and on September 1, 1982, I signed to the San Diego Padres as an amateur free agent. The skinny kid with a strong arm who might have died as a baby and who might have wasted his life in the streets was going to find out just how good he could be. It was up to me to show what I could do."

Jack McKeon, the man who gave the go-ahead to sign Benito, respected Luis Rosa's judgment and had come to Puerto Rico a few times. "Luis was a good scout for us, and we knew he would give us the cream of the crop of the kids. I'd been hearing about Benito and liked what I saw. After we signed him, we decided to start him out in Miami. Miami was an independent team then, and we had an arrangement with them as well as a couple of other teams. I thought it would be a good fit for Benny to be in a place with a fair-size Latin population that first year."

That wasn't something Benito expected, and as he was to discover, the next few years would be filled with situations he wasn't prepared for.

Chapter Two
Why You Can't Give Up

"You're so excited—thanks to God, you feel like it's the greatest thing in the world. Like somebody's handing you your dream. But the minors, it's tougher than anything you thought it would be. It's not like what you saw in your head."

For Benito, the thrill of signing his name to a contract with San Diego came with complications he neither anticipated nor fully comprehended as they unfolded. These were complications he could neither define nor articulate, yet they affected nearly a decade of the career he fought to achieve and hold on to.

"There was so much I didn't understand. If someone asked me if I understood, I always said, 'Yes' because if you don't, you think maybe you won't get to play baseball. My language was catching, hitting, the bat, the ball, and winning. This is what I knew, not enough English to communicate the right way. It wasn't something I could explain to people."

In looking back, Benito can see his struggles were as much about culture as language. If you draw an oval from Santa Isabel to Salinas, Ponce, Fajardo, and San Juan, it encompasses the northeastern and southeastern coastal parts of Puerto Rico, approximately a four-hour loop of driving on a day with light traffic. You can circumnavigate the entire island in approximately eight hours. Until he began playing in San Juan, Benito's world was the smaller twenty-mile radius of his town and those nearby. As an American territory, English is an official language as is Spanish in Puerto Rico, and while English is widely spoken in urban areas, the reality is in the 1990 U.S. Census, less than 20 percent of Puerto Ricans identified as being fluent in English. English is taught in the schools, but for many, the language outside those walls is Spanish. Benito had little interest in school, and with the decision to shoot for professional baseball at seventeen, his last thoughts were of formal education or what impact that could have compared to the raw talent he'd shown to men who could take him from the baseball fields of his youth to famous stadiums.

The strength of family and friends was something Benito took for granted as it is part of the heart of Puerto Rico. Go to any beach or park on a weekend and there will be large family groups everywhere, extended members and friends brought along, laughing, enjoying being together. Stores don't only close for major holidays—Easter, Mother's Day, and Father's Day are celebrated as well. Family time is held as more important than a day at the mall. In Benito's neighborhood and the surrounding towns, he was known and respected, his extraordinary ability a source of conversations in his parts of the island. He was greeted by name and congratulations almost everywhere he went. The impoverished nature of his upbringing meant there was little money; there was not, however, a lack of genuine warmth and affection among family and friends. Although millions of Puerto Ricans live in the United States, more than half reside in either the Northeast (predominantly New York) or the Southeast (predominantly Florida). Both these geographic areas allow easy return to Puerto Rico for individuals to visit family.

Benito, now among the thousands of hopefuls expecting to make it into the majors, was about to collide with more than a runner trying to make it to home plate. In realizing he was on his way, he recalled, "Before leaving, I had asked my father what he would advise me to do, and he told me that he was not the one who was going to go. I had to make the flight of six hours to San Diego alone, and I felt very helpless. I made the trip, and Jack McKeon was the Padres manager. I didn't know they were going to send me to Miami instead of staying in California, so it was funny in a way. I fly across the country that I've never done before and then back again to Florida; that's like only two hours flying from Puerto Rico. This was when the Miami International Single-A League was called the Miami Marlins, a few years before Miami was given an expansion team for the majors. At first, we stayed at a downtown hotel called the Columbus. I went in with five more players because we didn't have the money to pay unless we all stayed together. It was not in very good condition, and afterwards, we found an apartment with four to five players together to cover the monthly rent. It was on or close to Seventh Street, I think. We were charged around seven hundred dollars a month, but I only earned $271 every two weeks. We had no furniture, television, or even beds. We had nothing. For a long time, we had to sleep on the carpet, making a bed on the floor. One day I found a cot in the street someone had thrown out. I carried it home and slept on it. We were not eating very well because all the money went for the rent.

"But there was always something happening in downtown Miami; a lot of activity. The Latin heat is something that has always stayed with me, even though the time wasn't easy. It was more than me not understanding English. I didn't understand the culture either and hadn't expected it to be so different from Puerto Rico. San Juan is a big city, but it was nothing like being in Miami. Everything happened so fast. I was afraid to be there, and sometimes I cried in the dark because I felt so alone. I came from a very small place in Puerto Rico where I already knew everyone and I was celebrated wherever I went. Nobody was laughing at me, and nobody looked at me weird. In Miami, I noticed that some people looked at me with fear; that if I came along the sidewalk, they crossed the street and I didn't understand why. There were little things that tripped me up, too. Once I went out from the apartment to buy a Cuban sandwich and got lost. I couldn't remember how to get back, and all the buildings looked alike. I paced back and forth, and I finally sat on the sidewalk. Frustration was like a fire burning inside. After I thought I might go back to the store again, I looked across the street and finally recognized where to go. It was better for me to stay near the other players, and I left with them when we would go to eat because I didn't even know how to order food and all the food was rather unfamiliar for me, too. I felt very insecure. The only word I knew was 'hamburger,' but it came out as 'amburga.' I remember once when I had a milkshake and I wanted a straw. However it was I said it, they couldn't understand and finally handed me some packets of salt. There was a coffee shop that sold different food in front of the stadium, but all I ate there were burgers. To eat the kinds of things I was used to, I had to go to Latino places where I could order even though there weren't as many Latino places as there are today in Miami.

"I knew in a way this feeling of loneliness and frustration was going to cause problems in my relationships with managers and other players. I called my mother to send me a ticket to return to Puerto Rico. She told me no, that I should continue my career. I wasn't able to tell anyone else about how I felt.

"We played at the Field Maduro Stadium that has been replaced by condos, and many Latinos came to see me and cheer. This helped me feel more at home, like what I was used to. To be a good catcher, you must be well focused and concentrate on the game. All these distractions outside bothered me in the game, and that's just what I didn't want to happen. The game was so affected that I had to put all these emotions aside and really focus. To be a good catcher, you also have to learn around twelve signals and put 200 percent of the will into playing. If the game is lost, as soon as the game is over, you start thinking of the next one. Did you make a mistake today? How are you going to do it better? We played in the Florida State League, and that would take us to other places in Florida, too. Sometimes we traveled eight hours or more by bus.

"At the end of that first year, I was moved to Reno, Nevada and was still only nineteen. In leaving Miami, it meant I was being kept on in the minors, but there wasn't much Latino about Reno then and I had been learning more about baseball than English. Everyone had this idea that by being in Miami for a year, I must be able to understand everything going on, and it wasn't like that at all. 'Catcher, batter, and remove the runners to second' were what I knew and as much English as I could communicate, I could only express the basics to the pitcher.

"The worst part about Reno wasn't just that we had no money; it was the cold. I thought with Reno being in the desert it would be hot. I had never seen snow or been in cold like that. I didn't have a coat to keep me warm enough. Four of us shared a hotel, and without a car, we had to walk a mile to the stadium and then back. There were some times it snowed during the game and the locker room didn't have heat, so we waited until we walked to the hotel to shower. Trying to eat right was always a problem. Lucky for us, buffets in the casinos were really cheap at a couple of dollars, but most of our money was needed to pay for where we stayed. I would take two quarters and play a slot machine hoping to win three dollars so I could eat a big meal. I wouldn't try to play for more. I couldn't risk losing. As soon as I had a few dollars, I went straight to the buffet line to fill up.

"In going to the games, we had old school buses, and one time when it was really cold, a window was broken out, then when we were about an hour away from where we were supposed to play, the bus broke down. They couldn't get anyone out to fix it fast enough, and we all hitchhiked to get people to pick us up to get to the game.

"Reno was where I thought I couldn't take it anymore. Other guys had been dropping out and didn't make it even through the first year of the minors. I'm not talking about just Latinos like me who had trouble with the language. I mean guys from all over the country. They would quit and go home. The coaches never had to fire anyone because enough players dropped out on their own. It was one night when I was ready to give up, too. I called my mom and said I couldn't do this and wanted to come home. I know she loved me, but she said, 'You can come home, but you need to find out what you're going to do because this door will be closed to you. You won't be staying here.' I couldn't understand why she told me that at first, and after, I knew it was because she had faith in my talent, wanted me to be strong, and I stayed. Being in Reno was still super-tough, and it was important to make friends with people who I had never seen before. I was fortunate there were people who did reach out to help me by inviting me to their homes to sleep and eat because neither I nor my companions had anything. With my mom insisting I stick it out, having people like that made a big difference in how I started to feel. The next year when I was moved to Beaumont, Texas, to be in the Double-A League that meant my dream was another step closer. I really believed things couldn't be more difficult than in Reno, and I was right.

"The team was the Beaumont Golden Gators, and they had players like John Kruk, Roberto Alomar, Joey Cora, Ozzie Guillén, Sandy Alomar Jr., and Shane Mack. They weren't all there at the same time as me, but all these guys got called up to the majors, too. We played at the stadium of the college in town, and now we had nicer buses to ride in. Being in Double-A was where I was learning more English, mostly from watching TV when I could. It's hard to explain to people who think it's easy to learn a language if you've been living in places, but it wasn't like that for me. I could speak and understand more, but it isn't the same as being able to really get what people were saying or to express myself using the correct words.

"Meanwhile, Blanca, my girlfriend, was very, very happy but really didn't understand the way we had to make it through the minor leagues first, and as we passed that, she felt it was not a very easy life. Blanca and I were married February 12, 1985 in Puerto Rico. We found a judge; I used my brother's ring, and she used the ring of my brother's wife, Luis. After the judge announced us as married, we returned the rings. That was very funny, and it was sometime later before I could buy a ring for Blanca. There was no photographer so we had no photos of our wedding. There were six people at the ceremony and that was it. A little over a year later, our first child was born. I thought for sure it would be a boy, and, of course, he would be Benito Junior, so I started calling him 'Benny' before he was born. We were really surprised when it was a girl and decided to name her Bennybeth. You didn't get any kind of extra money in the minors if you had a family though. We didn't have a car, and it was too expensive to take a cab so when we got groceries I would push the grocery store cart and we would have to walk for two miles on the side of the street to get to the house. We had a lot of meals of nothing more than white rice and ketchup with a fried egg on top.

"Another part about being in the minors is you're playing at home maybe seven days and then on the road for nine or ten days. We spent four or five hours before the game to warm up, and you don't get time off while on the road. That's pretty much how it is for six months out of the year.

"After Beaumont, it was the Triple-A Pacific Coast League Las Vegas Stars. I was rising up in the minors. That didn't mean for sure I was going to make it, but I was working hard, showing what I could do, and getting stronger. Yeah, I was this skinny guy, but if you came close, you could see my arms were all muscle. Any runner trying to steal off me found out just how fast I could throw. One really special thing that happened was meeting Luis DeLeón. He was born in Ponce like me and was pitching with the Padres. He took me out for a steak, and I don't think I told him it was the first time I'd ever eaten a real steak in a restaurant. He talked to me about what it was going to be like when I got called up and shared his confidence that I would make it. I don't know if he'll ever understand how important he was to me at that time of my life. I remember he was in for a visit and we were watching when Pete Rose broke the record with 4,256 hits on September 11, 1985. That was a great experience for me. I mean I wasn't just watching back in a bar at home. I was playing in the minors, watching this moment with a man from my home who was a pitcher in the majors, telling me he thought I had the talent to go all the way. It was so exciting that I cried like a child."

Benito's steady progression through the minors did bring him a certain level of assurance about getting closer to the day he'd been dreaming of since he promised his mother he would be a star and buy her whatever she needed. The minor league system has its own unique history, and each year promising young players sign contracts. They either don't realize or don't acknowledge that almost 95 percent will never make the majors. Some are injured or develop health problems; others can't keep up the pace, can't adapt to the circumstances, or leave for myriad other reasons. Coaches and managers, many of whom came to baseball through the same route, are aware of the odds and can only allow so much sympathy. If a player doesn't have ambition to match physical talent, and can't cope with pressure, management might as well learn that before more money is invested. It's easier for Benito to look back at the system as a veteran player than when he watched teammates pack up and go home, anxiety battling with confidence that he was good enough to be in the small number targeted to advance to the ultimate prize.

"If you have no money and nothing to distract you, playing ball is all you do. You're more likely to focus on improving and learning the game. With no TV or money for other entertainment, you spend a lot of time thinking, 'Come on, Big Leagues, come on.' If you can stick through the tough parts, you're showing you're no quitter. Rookies earn a lot more now than when I came in. A big team knows what it's like coming up through Single-A, Double-A, and Triple-A, and they've been watching you all this time. They have a better idea of what they're paying for if you come through the minors. That doesn't mean the pay shouldn't be made some better for players, but guys like me never really had a chance to go to college. This was the only way to make it. I had been signed as a catcher, and sometimes, I would still joke about maybe I should be a shortstop instead. They sign you for a position, and they can change you after they watch you for a while, but they never talked about that with me. Catcher was what they meant for me to be."

The boy who had played in a field bordered by sugarcane on an island 3,200 miles away was on the verge of taking his biggest step yet. Perhaps one of the best "gifts" from his mentors was to introduce him to Scott Boras, an agent instantly recognizable in the major leagues. In September 1986, barely one year after watching Pete Rose's history-making hit, Benito and several other players were brought to San Diego. They were notable Triple-A players in the "Class of '86" who fans could watch and wonder if they were looking at the Padres' future. Benito's play may not have been flawless, but it was strong, and he was temporarily stunned after his initial showing.

"I only played like seventeen games and was told to go home. I couldn't understand it. They'd brought me up, I was here; I thought it was for real. I played well. What more did they want from me? Then I was told, 'No, Benny, you've got it all wrong.' What did I have wrong? I couldn't figure it out. What they explained was if I had played more games during that season, I wouldn't have been eligible to be a rookie in 1987. What they were offering me was the real thing, the move up to the majors I had been dreaming about. This time when I visited Puerto Rico, I could tell everyone I was going to be putting on the uniform of a catcher for the San Diego Padres. I had done it. I hadn't done it without the talent God gave me, faith of my family and friends, advice from my brothers, help from the men I've talked about, and a lot of hard work, but it was coming true. I was going to walk in the footsteps of the great Roberto Clemente and all my other baseball heroes."

Chapter Three
Catching the Dream

It was opening day for the San Diego Padres 1987, and Benito Santiago was suited up to squat behind the plate as a rookie in his own right. "I was there, in the same kind of position as Johnny Bench, Bob Boone, and Tony Peña—all catchers I had watched carefully on TV after I knew I was going to be a catcher. I was just twenty-two years old and had this great responsibility. The catcher is responsible for many things, being the manager of the game. To be a good catcher and call the game right, the catcher must know the pitcher very well and know what every particular pitcher brings to the game. You have to see the weaknesses of each pitcher and what his strengths are. The pitcher and catcher have to be together with good communication to work as a unit and try to think in the same way. It's also important to know the opposing pitcher and communicate with your team members so that everyone knows very well the strengths and weaknesses of the other team. You have to know what the situation is all the time. Every ballplayer has situations that appear in a game, and you have to point them out to the other team members so that everyone is reading the same book and coming together as a team, not as individuals.

"You also have to know nine-to-ten signals for communicating information. For example, they might want the pitcher to throw to first base or ask for a 'pitch-out.' That's when you throw outside of the hitter and get the ball to throw to second immediately—this would occur with fast runners who would have more of a chance to reach second. You learn pretty quick who those are and you watch and be ready. But this is the same time as you're watching the hitter. You have to see what both are doing. This is part of why I think baseball is one of the hardest sports to play well. There are multiple things going on all around, and you have only a second or sometimes less to react.

"The game is different in the first innings than at the end, and the pitcher has to control the game with the direction of the catcher. I always told the pitcher that what I do is, 'for your own good.' I was thinking and planning in advance in each game to know what would happen in the next two or three innings, especially when the batter reached first base. I had to know who followed in what order to plan how I was going to drive the game. For me, controlling the pitcher was the most important point in order to win the game. Also to manage the game, I had to learn a lot and know what to do when the pitcher wouldn't accept the signal. In my first couple of years, I didn't always know when a pitcher was tired . . . the communication between us had to be constant, and it was very important to know how he felt and what mood he was in.

"All this I was learning in that first season from 1987 to 1988. I wasn't always happy with my games. Like I had to check on my pitcher, to try and make him more aware of me and how I felt, and then there was how I had to behave with the rest of my teammates. The difference between the culture in which I grew up and culture of the United States and its various forms of behavior and 'signs' was confusing. Often I didn't react as I should have done, or I didn't know how to *be* what they were expecting me to be. Jack McKeon was the general manager in San Diego, and he helped a lot in integrating me into the game. He was the one who was there when I signed into the minors and was the one who sent me to Miami my first year. The new team manager was Larry Bowa, and I had a lot of respect for him, too. We had been in Triple-A together and beat Vancouver for the Pacific Coast League championship in 1986. He was a person who played very strong and something I learned from him was to play hard to develop in the game.

"Everybody wants to know about me throwing runners out from my knees, and it wasn't something I did right away in the majors. What happened was that I was playing well, but there were three runners I could never get out. One of them was Vince Coleman, and, man, I wanted to get him. He was with the Cardinals then and was known for his speed in stealing bases. He was the most exciting player when he was going to steal; he was that fast. I never saw anyone who was so quick; he would over-slide the base from being so fast.

"I remembered back to when I was maybe fifteen and was practicing with my brother Nelson. He said, 'Hey, try throwing from your knees at this can.' We had a trash can on the field, and I threw from my knees as hard as I could. I knocked that can a long way. Throwing from your knees wasn't something you were taught by the coaches, and I never tried it in front of them. I only did it the time with Nelson. Remembering about it made me think maybe that was the way to get Vince out. I knew I had to do it right though. If I made a throw like that in front of all the people and it didn't work, everyone would tell me it was a big mistake. They would wonder why I had such a crazy idea.

"What I did was I practiced in secret. When we were on the road, I would take a mattress from the bed and put it against the wall in the hotel so the sound wouldn't go to the next room. Then I would throw as hard as I could. The game came when I thought I was ready, and there Vince was, sure he could beat me to the base just like he had been doing. Ozzie Smith was one of the best shortstops I've ever seen in my life, and he had the best attitude as any player that I ever met. I was never on a team with him, but he was playing with Vince and the Cardinals. Ozzie was always talking smack about throwing players out, and it was the same for this game. Remember, I was going to maybe play shortstop if I hadn't become a catcher, and we were going back and forth about getting players out the whole time. I told Ozzie I had something special planned for Vince but didn't tell him what it was beforehand. It wasn't just that I didn't know for sure it would work. There was no way I wanted anyone to be ready for what I was going to do.

"My throw was exactly right, and when I got Vince out, everyone was going kind of crazy because I'd thrown from my knees. Like I said, I hadn't told anybody I was going to try this, and as soon as I went to the dugout, I said to the manager, 'Don't worry, I won't do that again.' He looks at me and said, 'It's okay; I like it. You throw like that any time you want to.' I think Vince was mad at me that first time because it was something so different than what he expected. Ozzie loved it, but Vince was taken by surprise. It was priceless.

"The fans they would all yell out at every game after that, 'Throw from your knees, Benny!' They didn't understand I had to make a decision each time about which way to throw. Tony Peña used to throw players out from home to first from his knees, but never as far as second. I studied him, and that helped me figure out how I was going make the throw to second. I kept practicing for about a month to get even better from my knees, but you have to see where the ball goes, too. I paid attention to the players, and if there was a really fast runner, it was usually quicker for me to get the ball off from my knees than my pop time to standing. But if the pitch was too high or too far to either side, I would have to reach too far out and wouldn't have the right balance. If I knew I could get the runner out from standing, I would do that. I liked having the fans cheer, but winning was the most important thing. All these decisions, you have to make really fast and I had to be good whichever way I threw. That's why my strong arm was so important."

Austin Wasserman, owner/co-founder and director of strength and conditioning at A.B. Athletic Development and founder of WassermanStrength.com, wrote a lengthy explanation of Benito's throwing ability from a standing position. The explanation of technique was combined with a video clip of his motions. You can imagine the movements with Mr. Wasserman's vivid imagery.

Benito Santiago was one of the best throwing catchers to play the game. Santiago is best known for throwing runners out from his knees. Watch the hip to trunk relationship during this throw as well as the arm pattern while his body moves forward toward the target.

Santiago starts with his back foot on the ground (knee flexed) and the lead leg or 'shin' on the ground (again lead knee is flexed), with the lead leg further in front toward the target. His hips will extend in order to move the trunk into an upright position. Even though his trunk is upright, it is still turned back against his hips! He does this by activating the glute musculature. Remember that the glutes, when activated or squeezed, extend the hips. When throwing, the hips will move from flexion into extension by the activation of the glute musculature. This also creates velocity!

As the hips become extended, there is back leg femoral movement. The hips are opening up while the trunk is still closed and turned back against the hips. The femur is internally rotating in the acetabulum (hip socket) as the trunk turns back against the hips. As you can see, he ends up kneeling down to throw this ball, so there is no formal stride pattern. The right knee is already flexed (bent), so the knee cannot be initiating the back leg movement as so many coaches instruct. The femur is actually moving in the hip joint as it would in a normal step and throw movement. The lead leg will externally rotate as it would in a normal stride pattern.

You can see the lead leg externally rotates and lands on the knee as the arm starts to move through external rotation. This lead leg external rotation is the same movement that would happen in a normal stride. At ball release there will be a sudden stop of that lead leg movement, and the body will 'pop' up slightly. This is the body decelerating after the throw. The right leg will come forward just as it would in a normal step-and-throw follow-through.

As mentioned above, the hips are opening up as the trunk is turning back against the hips. The trunk also maintains that 'turn' until the arm moves through its necessary pattern. This is how resistance is created! You can also see that the hips are moving into extension, from glute activation, which is also how velocity is created.

As the arm moves through its proper pattern into and through external rotation, the hips are opening up and the trunk is turning or already is turned back against those opening hips. The trunk will then release in the transverse plane and fire toward the target, bringing the arm forward to ball release. In order to create velocity, you must create resistance in a throw! The clip above shows exactly how resistance is created between the hips and trunk. This overlapping movement must happen in order to maximize throwing potential.

(The post with video can be seen at https://wassermanstrength.com/high-level-throwing-benito-santiago/#comment-80061)

Benito's reputation—based on his dependable arm and what became his "logo" of throwing runners out from his knees—was enhanced by a string of hits that gave him a .300 average for the season and a record of hitting safely in thirty-four straight games. At the time, it set multiple records because it was the longest hitting streak for a Padres player, a rookie, a Latin, and a catcher. Each consecutive game that built toward the record brought extra press attention. This was the sort of encounter that could cut both ways. Benito easily recalls the day the streak came to an end.

"I had gone into the locker room and they came to get me and said, 'Benny, get out here. People want to see you,' and I wasn't sure what they meant. I went back on the field, and there were lots of fans cheering, calling my name, and they put a flag of Puerto Rico right onto the field. It felt so good to see that and hear them. They gave me a standing ovation that lasted, like, ten minutes.

"Then everyone wanted to talk to me, lots of press and photographers, and I go into this room that was full of people. I had just finished the game, and I don't know what it is I am supposed to say; nobody told me. Everyone thinks it's easy to answer, to tell them how I feel, but it wasn't. I didn't want to say something wrong and then see the next day in the paper or hear on the TV that I made a mistake with words or used an expression the wrong way. I tried not to say too much, and nobody saw how nervous I was."

There was an ironic twist to his streak though. "I had no idea when my streak would end. Every time I got up to bat, it might have been that day, but I kept getting hits. So what happened was, I broke the streak in the last game at the end of the season, and then the next season, I started off with fifteen hits in a row. If I had made that thirty-fifth game, the streak would have officially been extended into the new season, and I would have finished with fifty instead. Think about that—one hit made the difference, but I didn't realize it until later. I mean, I didn't know I would have a short streak in '88, so maybe I wouldn't have concentrated more for that thirty-fifth game, but I still wonder about it sometimes. Thirty-four was a record for sure, but, man, wouldn't fifty have been something?"

With that said, Benito rightfully remembers the multiple thrills of 1987. "It was really good year for me, even more than I had hoped for. I was Rookie of the Year, and I won Silver Slugger for my hitting. What was hard for me to believe sometimes was these catchers who were famous with other teams, they would talk to me, too, and give me advice about how I was playing, about what it was like to be a catcher. These were guys I had seen on TV when I was growing up, and now I was one of them. It was my dream coming true. I wasn't happy about my game unless we won, and I was always thinking about what to do better. My whole life was about baseball, and for me it would be forever, I thought. It's no coincidence that a lot of general managers and managers in the big leagues began their careers as catchers. There was Mike Scioscia, Tony Peña, Bruce Bochy, and Joe Girardi. That could be me some day. I was proving myself, and it was still hard for me with the English, not understanding the way I wanted to and especially not being able to use the right words at times. The hardest part was other people always thinking I could understand, and it wasn't that way. I didn't know how to explain it. Being outside of Puerto Rico, I still felt very insecure, but I was playing well and that was the important part. By the end of the season, there were some runners who stopped trying to steal because they knew they couldn't beat me."

While the competitive world of major league baseball wasn't ready to anoint twenty-two-year-old Benito as a future Hall of Famer, there was no question that he was a rising star to be watched. He was well past being a "Cup of Coffee" player [the unfortunate guys who had one game in the majors and disappeared]. In fact, when Benito was named Rookie of the Year by the Baseball Writers' Association of America, it was unanimous and only the fifth unanimous pick in the thirty-eight-year history of the National League award. How much he would improve and how long he could last at the demanding position were the questions to be answered.

With the 1987 season over, Benito returned to Puerto Rico, where his family, friends, neighbors, and thousands of baseball fans expressed their pride in him. Yet, their world hadn't changed in the way his had. It wasn't as if he retreated into a peaceful estate or jetted away on a luxury vacation. The streets were as tough as ever, the neighborhood was still where people lived with little money, and he slipped back into speaking far more Spanish than English. He kept himself in shape, talked a lot with his former coaches, signed autographs for eager kids, and hadn't yet come to think of California as his home.

Chapter Four
A Coveted Cover Photo

Despite the early hitting streak, Benito's batting settled in at .248, and even though he was represented by Scott Boras, one of the most powerful agents in baseball, there were times when he felt he wasn't as valued by his team as he should have been. And yeah, there were sporadic angry outbursts, too, that fellow players like Jack Clark cautioned him against. He did what he'd always done and focused on his skills to express how much the game meant to him.

"I was a good guy, and winning was what I wanted, but I still couldn't explain in a way to make everyone understand me. I didn't have the words to say it right. It would make me mad to lose a game. I would be trying to make the point about why I was mad, and it wouldn't come out right, or I wouldn't understand what kind of point someone was trying to make with me. There was one time Jack McKeon is yelling at me, and he said, 'You need to grow up.' I'm thinking to myself, 'Grow up? I'm six-one. How much more does he want me to grow?' I didn't get what he was trying to tell me. But if I had said that to him, he probably would have thought I was making a joke. So he's mad, I'm mad, and neither of us knows we don't understand each other. The reporters are always around and asking how you're feeling after a game. Sometimes I would shoot words out right after we lost, and the press would make them sound worse than what I really meant. They were just doing their job, and it made for a good story from their point of view. Now that I'm older, I realize I should have worked harder at getting better about how to say things to reporters. When you're trying to make the majors, you worry about how you play and don't think about stuff like how you're going to sound to the press. It's like in that movie, *Bull Durham*. Most baseball movies don't get it right, but that guy Kevin Costner, he's good with them. Have you seen it? You know the part I'm talking about? Where the catcher is explaining about reporters to the pitcher?"

Yes, indeed. In the movie, Costner plays the role of Crash Davis, a catcher in the minors who had a brief time in the majors. He's been brought on to the Bulls team to try to help shape a young pitcher, Ebby Calvin "Nuke" LaLoosh, played by Tim Robbins. Nuke has plenty of talent but lacks discipline in the way he pitches. There are several humorous scenes, and fairly late in the movie, Crash says something like, "It's time to work on your sports clichés. Write these down." Nuke doesn't understand. Crash tells him that when he's successful, he'll have reporters sticking microphones in front of his face and if he has the right clichés ready, he won't make a mistake and say the wrong thing. Then Crash goes through several statements like, "You have to play them one at a time," and so forth. In one of the closing scenes, you see Nuke, who has been brought up to the majors, repeating back what he had practiced to a pretty reporter.

Benito nodded. "Kevin Costner makes it funny in the movie. It wasn't so funny in real life when I used words I shouldn't have, and it made me look like I didn't care about my teammates or the fans. I can't change what I did, but guys can learn from me."

Not that 1988 wasn't a good year. Roberto Alomar, a fellow Puerto Rican was on the team, and they were able to talk about home and what it was like to have come from the small, closely knit island to a city like San Diego. Benito snagged another Silver Slugger Award and a Gold Glove. It also was the year that he led all league catchers in throwing out base runners by throwing 44.7 percent of them out. On the personal side, even if the money wasn't as much as he felt he should have received, the six-figure salary he had once dreamed of was a reality. He was finally able to think about buying a house, and he did buy a BMW as his first of what would be a string of luxury cars to follow.

Physically, he understood the power in his throws might be a gift, but keeping in shape was a daily task. At six-foot one-inch and 180 pounds, he was lean to the point some called skinny, and that had more than one advantage for him. "Keeping my weight right was part of how I could extend my time as a catcher. It's harder on your knees you start carrying around extra weight. I wanted to play all the time, every game, and the way to do that was show them I wasn't tired. I didn't want to sit out. Not me, not like some of the other catchers. You don't play, why do they need you? That's why I tell the second catcher he won't be playing much and get used to it. We had one who said to me, 'Hey, Benny, I got to play a whole ten games this season. How do you expect me to get a raise with that?' I told him that was just the way things were going to be if he stayed around me."

During off-season, Benito continued to live between his two worlds with strong ties to the rough neighborhood where he grew up, going for weeks with little English spoken around him and everyone in Puerto Rico knowing his name. Among the visits he made was to a man he admired who hadn't pulled away from drugs and violence. He was in prison convicted of quadruple homicides. Was he guilty, or had he been the most convenient suspect? They'd grown up together, and as teenagers, he was in the circle of people who'd insisted Benito wasn't to waste his talent. He'd helped convince Benito to follow baseball as his true path and now wouldn't hear of Benito trying to help his situation. His friend told him, "People outside won't understand if you take up for me. They won't understand you're trying to help because of how we were as kids. They'll make a big deal out of you being friends with someone convicted of murder and make it look bad. You have too much going for you. I won't let you do this."

Benito recognized and accepted the harsh truth. Too many boys and teens he'd grown up with were dead or serving prison sentences. His brother, this friend, and others had intervened when he was young to pull him away from the same potential fate, and they wanted to see him succeed. For them, his accomplishments were something they could also be a part of, knowing the role they had played in his early life. Every award he earned proved they had been right about how special he was.

His old coach, Angel Cruz, could attest to that. When Benito left to go through the challenging years of the minors, he'd told Angel he would not forget the teams in Santa Isabel and Jauca. Benito kept his promise, and as the man who had persevered and made it to the majors, he came back with new uniforms and equipment to outfit the teams.

In the world of professional baseball Benito had fought to be a part of, his third season awaited and with it came two events players remember forever. The Special Edition *Sports Illustrated* April 5, 1989, "Catch a Rising Star," came out with Benito's photograph on the cover and in lower type, "San Diego's Benito Santiago, Best of a Rare Breed."

He topped that by being named to his first Major League Baseball All-Star Game, and for Benito, there could be no question he was where he belonged. "It was July 11, 1989, at Anaheim Stadium where I heard the national anthem of the United States as the president of the United States, President Bush, stood in the same baseball field with me. President Ronald Reagan announced some of the game. It was the second time I had seen Reagan. The first time was in the locker room at an opening day game, and I was so nervous to be around him that I couldn't talk.

"I also met many outstanding players like Nolan Ryan, Jack Clark, Tony Gwynn, Wade Boggs, Bo Jackson, Mike Scioscia, Ozzie Smith, and many other very famous players I had seen as a child in Puerto Rico. I considered it an honor I never dreamed of. More than sixty-four thousand people had come to watch the game, and I had been chosen by the fans to be receiving or 'catcher.' It was not bad thing for a Puerto Rican boy who almost died at three months of age. My family that had adopted me all came to the game—my parents, my siblings, my wife, and my children. My mother was sitting behind home plate. We traveled from San Diego to Anaheim in a limousine and stayed at the Disneyland Hotel."

It was an exciting game for the crowd as well. Disney characters paraded onto the field for the opening, and the popular Doc Severinsen led *The Tonight Show* orchestra in playing the American and Canadian national anthems. President Reagan, who once had a career as a baseball announcer, had been invited to come into the booth with Vin Scully to help call the first inning. From a playing perspective, Bo Jackson was the center of attention. The talented athlete who played professional baseball for three different teams and spent four seasons with the Los Angeles Raiders professional football team was at the top of his game that day and was awarded Most Valuable Player.

Benito remembered Jackson for his own reason. "As a catcher, I made it a point to almost never step away from any runner. They hit you and make you drop the ball, they're safe. With my long arms and being quick, I could usually tag them without blocking the plate. The really big guys, though, they could and would hurt you and they would charge on in. Bo Jackson, this is a guy who takes down football players, and he's got twenty or thirty pounds on me. You let him hit you, and you're lucky if you don't get hurt badly. I couldn't take a chance like that. I watched Pete Rose take out a catcher in an All-Star Game, and I didn't want the same thing to happen to me."

For Benito, what more could the Padres ask of him? His hitting might not be as strong as his rookie year, but it was still a benefit for the team. Besides, he hadn't been signed for his ability at bat. "It took me some time to accept as much as I liked getting a home run, I was more an RBI guy, and even if I had a great day of hitting, if we lost the game, it didn't help the team. Other players could make runs, but not many of them could get guys out like I could. Learning how to put my focus there was the most important part, aside from managing the pitcher.

"Like I said before, one of the reasons professional baseball is so hard to play is you have more than one thing going on at a time and it can be happening quickly. If a batter gets a hit and you have a runner on first, you have to be ready for maybe the chance at a double play. If there's a runner on third, I have to be ready for him, too, but if they're already down two outs, you take whatever the best chance is for an out. You have to know where the ball is all the time. Instead of trying to watch all the players, you keep fixed on the ball and learn to count for the runners. You learn who's fast and who's not and about how many seconds it will take to get between bases depending on the usual speed of the runner. That way, you know you have a certain amount of time before you have to shift your body to a new direction or stance. It's an awareness you develop. Some of the older catchers, they can explain these tricks to you. You have to be willing to listen, practice, and keep your mind on the game."

Former baseball stars weren't the only ones who could give Benito advice. "In San Diego, the team members made a lot of charity appearances, and there would be different celebrities around depending on what the event was. There was the time I met with Muhammad Ali. I don't remember the exact date, but Reagan was president. When Ali came into the room, everyone stood up and clapped. I was a kid when he was really at his peak, and at first I wondered who this man was because he was older and I wasn't expecting it to be him. I was so intimidated when they told me who he was that I couldn't get words out. Muhammad Ali did more than just shake your hand like most guys do when they don't know you. He would make you talk to him. He was more aggressive as far as getting you to talk to him even though he couldn't speak Spanish. He didn't allow me to just stand there. One thing he told me was to have fun with the game, and after I played nine innings, I'd see what the results were. I had to have a translator, and I asked him why, and he said that's what he did in boxing and if I did the same thing in baseball, I would be the same as him. I listened to what he said, and he was honest, and he was right about it. But when I talked to someone like that, I didn't really understand the value of what he was telling me until years later. I admired him so much. No question in my mind that he was the best athlete in the world. I have a photo of him, but I can't find it now. I hope I haven't lost it."

During the 1989 season, league catchers were credited with twenty-eight pickoffs of base runners, and fourteen of those belonged to Benito. As his reputation for throwing with speed and from awkward positions became recognized, there was no question runners and their coaches thought carefully before trying to steal off him. "The players, they would say to me, 'Hey, Benny, you're going to throw your arm out someday; you should take it easy.' I tell them, you worried about my arm, you stay on base and I don't have to throw so hard. You think you can steal, and I'm going to get you out.

"The other thing about baseball is you're on the road so much of the year, but you go to places like New York City where there is all this history of baseball. It was the place where everyone in the world wanted to go. I was kind of surprised with mixed feelings because I was disappointed in how the city looked because of the drunks around, and the dirt and stuff. It wasn't what I expected at all, but even with that, it was also the most interesting place in the world. As a kid, I don't know how many games I watched being played from Shea Stadium and now it was me in a uniform on the field. For me, it was an honor to play against New York because of the tradition. You see some of the landmarks your first time like the Twin Towers that were really impressive, and they've done a lot to make the city nicer. There's so much to love about the city. I had been told I had to watch out in New York, but the people were great there and gave me a lot of love. There are so many Puerto Ricans and Latinos you expect that because that's how we are; we show our pride. I enjoy all the fans, but it's special to have a lot of Puerto Ricans there to watch me. It was more than just another stadium, and my playing was exciting at that time. Like everywhere, when I threw from my knees, they loved it, and off the field, they embraced me. I was a hero there. I have to say it's one of the best towns I ever played in, and I spent a lot of money there. You can buy anything, and there are so many places to go out to. At first, I didn't go out much; I mostly stayed in my room. Eventually, over time, I started coming out of my room as I got to know people from my hometown or from Puerto Rico. The Latino community is strong, and people treated me as if I was their son. It didn't matter Puerto Rico, the Dominican, Cuba—they are all Latino countries that love baseball and they made me feel welcome.

"Other guys knew the city better—Howard Johnson and Gary Carter with the Mets; Kevin Mitchell, who was my neighbor in San Diego; Keith Hernandez; and Lenny Dykstra. I got to know them, and we would talk at the stadium about where to go and what to do. The thing is, though, you do have to be careful in New York because it is easy to get into trouble. You take a player like Derek Jeter. I remember when he reached three thousand hits and you have to admire him as a special player. He spent his entire career there, kept himself clean, and didn't have any kind of big problems with the press or being out in nightclubs and that kind of thing."

There was one particular trip to New York, though, that impacted Benito's life in a completely unexpected way. He was at his hotel and answered a knock at the door. "I look out, and there are these women. I don't know them, and I ask what's going on. I was thinking it's some kind of a joke guys are playing on me. Guys do stuff like that all the time. They said, 'We're your sisters, and we want to see you,' and this doesn't make sense. They're telling me they're my sisters from the family in Puerto Rico that I was born into, not the family I grew up with. I got on the phone quick to my mom—my mom Nelida who raised me. Thank God she was there to take my call, and she said they were my sisters all right, the ones I never knew anything about. That was the last thing I thought would happen to me. When I was in the court as a kid and the judge was making the decision about which family I would live with, I didn't want to know my other family because I wanted to stay with the Gonzales. After it was over, I put them out of my mind and they didn't try to see me again either."

"It was hard to explain how weird this all was. I mean I'm in town for a baseball game, and with no warning, I find out I have some family living in New York in the Bronx. We talked for a while and said we would maybe get together again before too long."

What did they want from him, and how was he supposed to feel about them? It would take time to sort through what, if any, kind of relationship he was to have with his birth family. "It wasn't all at once I could be with them. It wasn't until later I went to visit them and my brother, who didn't come with them that first time."

Chapter Five
The True Price of a Lamborghini

"Two hundred and forty-five thousand dollars. Who needs to pay a price like that for a car? And it wasn't just the Lamborghini. I had a Porsche, BMW, Ferrari—this is what I mean. The cars, the clothes, I wanted them; I bought them. I had made it, and I thought it was going to last my whole career. My agent, Scott Boras, tried to tell me this wasn't the way to handle my money, and I didn't want to listen to him. He had seen it happen plenty of times, but I didn't think what he was warning me about was meant for me."

Benito had at least taken his agent's advice to buy a house near San Diego, a symbol of stability instead of flamboyance. Scott Boras had also traveled to Puerto Rico trying to understand the roots of the volatility Benito too often exhibited. Benito's reputation for making comments like 'They stink,' in describing the pitching staff, didn't help when they went into negotiations. Decisions about keeping players can be a complex mix, and a short fuse that flares into anger in the locker room can be viewed as troublesome. One particular day was the worst incident. "You know, I don't even remember exactly why, but I got so mad at McKeon—the guy I owed almost everything to— and I felt like I wanted to grab him by the shirt and push him up against the lockers. It was crazy of me, and I don't know what all I said to him being as mad as I was. As soon as I calmed down enough to leave the clubhouse, I was sure it was the end for me. It should have been, with me acting the way I had. I got into the car where my mom was waiting, and I told her I think I'll be off the team. The very next day I woke up around 6:00 a.m., expecting to see in the newspapers that I had been released. McKeon didn't do that; he kept it private and didn't talk to reporters or anyone else. If it hadn't been for him, my career would have been over then. He's a great guy, and if I had listened more to him when I was younger, I might have been better as a team member—not playing, my playing was never the problem—it was how to react to things, how to manage things. What a great man he is, one of the best leaders in baseball."

Coach McKeon was no stranger to players who lost their tempers. "I wouldn't say Benny was exactly a hothead, but yeah, he'd get mad about different things. If I benched him, he'd start up about it. I'd tell the guy he couldn't play all 162 games, and at the time, he couldn't understand when I wanted to pull him. After a while, Jack Clark came to me and asked to be moved so his locker was next to Benny. Jack said he'd been a lot like him when he was young, and he thought he could help settle Benny down and I think he did. It takes time for young players to mature, to learn that when certain decisions are made, it's usually for their own good."

The maturing process was only one piece of the puzzle. It was true that Benito was not the only baseball player who had endured poverty and a violence-ridden upbringing. Yet, the loss of a father he'd never had the chance to love, the haunting question of why an entire family would give him away, and the sudden reappearance of members of that same family were not issues he would discuss with fellow players, even if he had the English skills to do so.

"People would notice the big tattoo of my dad, Jose, on my arm, and there was a long time when I would buy a seat for him while I was with San Diego because I wanted to feel that he was there with me." This wasn't something he wanted to explain to other people either.

After seeing the environment of those hard streets and learning more about the unusual circumstances of his youth, Boras carefully broached the subject of trying some sessions with a psychologist. For Benito, it was a solution he had never considered. "She was from Argentina so language wasn't a problem. She was good to talk to, a smart lady. I saw her for a while, and it helped me understand better how to work with my teammates. She let me see things I hadn't been able to make sense of. She wanted me to see there were other ways to deal with frustration than being angry."

After the birth of Benito Junior, Benito's adopted mother, Nelida, decided to move in with them to make life easier for Benito's wife who had difficulty coping with her husband's frequent absences. The Gonzalez children were all grown, and Nelida's husband accepted her reasoning about why she felt her presence around Benito could have a positive effect. Games on the road created stress—all the late nights partying were Benito's choice and caused friction that increasingly escalated into quarrels. If he couldn't see the need to be there more for his wife, at least there would be someone sympathetic at home to help with the demands of two young children as well as reduce the sense of isolation for what was still a young woman who was also far from her own extended family.

Angry outbursts around his teammates did lessen, but not the intensity of his play as more awards came. He earned his third Gold Glove in 1990, third and fourth Silver Slugger in 1990 and 1991, and three more All-Star appearances in 1990, 1991, and 1992. Benito's first significant injury in the majors prevented him from playing in the 1990 All-Star game. "I took a ball to my ribs, then it hit my hand and broke the outside bone of my thumb. I was on the injured list for almost three months. I had to expect to be injured at some point, but I wish it had hadn't kept me out of the game. It's such a special thing to be part of."

Benito hated missing the 1990 All-Star Game; he enjoyed both the competitive play and all the hoopla that accompanied such a glittering event. His career gave him opportunities he never dreamed of as a poor kid in Puerto Rico, the chance to meet presidents and socialize with Hollywood celebrities. He enjoyed seeing President Ronald Reagan at an All-Star Game. "I also met Presidents Clinton and George Bush Senior at All- Star Games. We had time to spend about ten to fifteen minutes talking to them. I was really honored to meet them, and I was able to get a photo with them.

"While playing for the Padres, during spring training, Bob Hope invited several players to his house. I was impressed by his helicopter pad on top of his house, and it was a palace. His house was in a private neighborhood, and at that moment, I could appreciate how famous Bob Hope was.

"You have all this amazing stuff going on in your life, and you can't see it might end someday. Baseball was everything to me; it was what drove me. I had to keep being the best I could, and I was put together with a special trainer who had a workout system that at first didn't make sense to me. He takes me to the track. I play baseball, not track, and he tells me to run 100s, 200s, and I'm thinking this is a little crazy. I was sore the next day like I had never been. He keeps working with me, though, to build up my endurance, and after a while, I could tell the difference. I would finish nine innings and be ready to do more. 'Let's have a doubleheader' was what I said sometimes after the game.

"I kept telling them they don't need to spend money to bring other catchers in because I was going to be the one playing. The year when I played 152 games was the only time I said it might be too much. I was good for 135–140 or so and that's more than most catchers. Pitchers, they rotate them to where they are only pitching every three to four days and even less now. And on some days when I was supposed to be off, I would play third base. For me, it was the same as having a day off. I wasn't wearing the equipment, I wasn't in the crouch position or moving up and down all game, and if we were playing at our best, runners didn't make it past second base. Most guys don't hit to third base. That's how you know if a catcher is slowing down—you see him playing third base a lot."

For Benito, what he had to give and what he was giving should have placed him in the same category of his teammates who were receiving multiyear contracts. "Guys around me, they were making more money and getting longer contracts. I wanted to stay in San Diego, but they were wrong to think they could keep me without paying what I deserved."

The arbitration result of $1.65 million in 1991 as a settled amount in his contract dispute wasn't what he was looking for, and Benito was coming up as a free agent. California may have given him his first chance at his dream, but there were other teams where his skills could be appreciated. San Diego was his home, where he wanted to be. The multiyear contract he asked for was once again refused by the Padres. The result of the next arbitration was very different, however, as his agent Scott Boras refuted any idea Benito was slipping. The end result of the facts he laid out during negotiations was a telephone call to Benito giving him the news he had just become the highest paid catcher in baseball history with a $3.3 million award. He went on to be selected to his fourth All-Star Game in what ironically turned out to be his last season with the Padres. Suddenly, boos were more frequent from the fans than the cheers of his earlier seasons. As had happened in the past, remarks he made to reporters about fans not understanding baseball and his sharp opinion about the pitchers and managers were words he probably shouldn't have spoken out loud, even if he didn't intend for them to be insulting.

His name in the press wasn't limited to his performance on the field. There was a late-night traffic stop that escalated to a run-in with the police that landed him in jail for several hours as possible charges were discussed. It was almost a month before everything was dismissed, and speculation about what had happened and how it might affect his career quickly spread. True fans sided with Benito's explanation of a misunderstanding blown out of proportion. Others took a dimmer view and even his hometown papers in Puerto Rico voiced their disapproval. It was hard on him, and his own feelings about staying in San Diego were brought into conflict. Although he knew he could overcome the incident, how much did he want to change and give in rather than make a new start somewhere else?

He reached the point where he was philosophical about the situation and the Padres balking at paying him what he was asking for. "It's all about business. Baseball is a passion, a way of life for me since I was a kid, but it's a business. Things don't always go the way you plan or how you want."

Was the money not there as management claimed, or were they simply not willing to acknowledge Benito as they did others? For Benito, it was their choice, and it was time to move on. "In looking back, I don't know, maybe I should have been willing to do some things differently. It's hard to know if I could have."

At this stage, family and baseball clashed more sharply than in the past. His wife, Blanca, had finally comfortably settled into the area. Their daughter was in a daycare she liked; their son was a toddler. How was she supposed to pick up and move when there was no indication life with a man who seemed to care more about baseball and partying than being with his family would be different? The fabric of what had become a frayed marriage tore. With the divorce, his wife planned to stay in California for at least a while.

Benito was committed to taking care of his family, which would now be on the opposite coast. "I always made sure they had money—I would never deny that to my family, and I didn't try to play any kind of tricks with the settlement. I didn't want the divorce, and I couldn't see why it had to happen. This is one of the things all the fame and attention does to you. It makes you think whatever you want is the most important and all that matters. You go places and people tell you how great you are. They want your autograph, want to have a photo with you, want to be with you. You think that can take the place of a family and real friends who are with you as a person instead of just wanting to hang around a celebrity. I couldn't see the truth of that until much later, when I realized I hadn't been the husband and father I should have been. I can't change how I acted during that time, but I can tell young kids how easy it is to make those mistakes. I hope they learn from me."

Chapter Six
Back to Miami

The distance between San Diego and Miami is a little over 2,650 miles. From a personal perspective, though, Benito's return to Miami might as well have been an entire world away. The skinny teenager who was broke and only one of thousands of young baseball hopefuls was now twenty-eight with a string of awards and a $7.2 million two-year contract to show how far above being "just another hopeful" he was. "Being in Miami was good, too, because of being closer to Puerto Rico and with all the Latinos. Most of those young players hadn't seen me play in San Diego, so they were excited to see me play the way I did. In 1993 when I came, it was so much fun—fun for the fans to have a major league team. They always wanted to see me throw from my knees—it's like they didn't care about anything else. They ask how do you do it, and I tell them it's just how I am, something I can do, my logo, and what almost everyone remembers.

"There are plenty of celebrities who live or spend time in Miami and I met Andy García, the actor, who made it a point to stop by the clubhouse in Miami to see me and later when I was in San Francisco. We became friends, and it was an honor to me to meet him and get to know him. Later, after I was in San Francisco, there was one time at a game when Andy was cold in the stands and I gave him a Giants jacket to wear. He would always love Miami, but he was a Giants fan that day when he wore the jacket."

It was indeed an exhilarating time in Miami for anyone who loved baseball. One of two cities awarded Major League expansion teams in 1991, Miami had selected its team in the 1992 draft, and adding four-time All-Star Benito as catcher gave them defensive depth. "Sure, I wanted to stay in San Diego if things had been different, but you can't let what happened on one team stay with you. It's baseball, and once you leave a team, you leave. You can have friends and like to see them again, but I'm always out there to win. The first time you go against your former team, it can seem kind of strange, but for me as a catcher, there is an advantage. I know how everyone hits, I know what their weak spots are, and I can signal the pitcher what to throw."

The Marlins might not have a brand-new stadium like Baltimore's Camden Yards, but when Joe Robbie Stadium was built, multiuse facilities were common and it was designed to handle baseball as well as the Miami Dolphins football games. In preparation for the Marlins' debut, several million dollars had been spent getting ready for more than forty-two thousand fans who would pour through the gates and into their seats on Opening Day. Rain had been pouring as well the morning of April 5, 1993, and it's hard to know how many pleas were made to Mother Nature asking for a break.

The same pleas were followed by fervent thanks as the clouds did clear and Opening Day souvenirs sold out with fans expressing their confidence in the new Marlins team poised to come up against the Los Angeles Dodgers. At age seventy-eight, baseball legend Joe DiMaggio threw the first ball out, and World Series veteran pitcher Charlie Hough was in sync with Benito. "What a great day that was for us. So much excitement. It was extra special to have been in Miami with the minors, now to be there for the first time to have a professional team. You can't ever know for sure you're going to win a game, but it felt right for that one."

Hough struck out the first two batters to set the rhythm for the game. Second baseman Bret Barberie got the first hit for the team, and Benito came in with a run. Dodger Tim Wallach did blast a home run into the stands, but later rookie center fielder Scott Pose had a save with the kind of spectacular catch that brought the crowd to its feet. By the ninth inning, almost no one was sitting and waves of cheers and hoarse screams greeted the Marlins 6-3 win.

Even though more than three million attendees were part of the thrill of the season, hometown fans didn't get the joy of seeing the first Marlin home run being hit in their own stadium. That came a week after the opening game win. It was San Francisco on April 12, 1993, as the catcher who had been brought in for his defensive ability made a hit he would long remember.

"I felt good going up to the plate," Benito recalled. With one runner on base, Benito sent the ball flying and brought them both in to score. [The segment was captured and can be found on YouTube.] It was his first home run of the season, and he would make another dozen.

"One of the best players for the Marlins was Andre Dawson. He had one of the best swings in baseball. I had actually met him in my rookie year when he was playing for Chicago and I was with the Padres. I was catching and he got hit in the head. I asked him how he was and thought he would be mad, but he wasn't. He was always a gentleman. It wasn't until afterwards I found out how good he really was. I came to the Marlins and had a chance to see how he was always helping out other players. He was a role model to a lot of us and became a major influence on my style. I changed some of my habits because I watched him, admired his batting style, and he took time to explain his methods."

No matter how much enthusiasm is generated, it isn't likely for an expansion team to make the play-offs their first year, and with a 64-98 record, the Marlins were no exception. "I had some bad habits I let get out of hand," Benito said after having such a promising start to the season. "There were lots of people around to party with. Man, you get caught up in that, and you don't think the way you should. I had people coming to the house I didn't even know—the kind that wanted to be able to say they hung out with me. You have money, and you like to spend it—nice clothes, jewelry, always the cars. You're out on the town throwing it around. There were other things going on in my head, too, and my game wasn't where I wanted it to be or where it should have been." He dropped to .230 in hitting, and his unerring ability to throw out base runners nudged in under 30 percent. Frustration with himself and criticism inside the locker room too often burst into angry responses with teammates, coaches, and sometimes reporters.

During the winter, Nelida Gonzalez, the woman who would always be Benito's mother, decided she had kept silent long enough. "This is the woman who knows me like nobody else. She's the one who wouldn't let me quit when I wanted to come home from the minors, and now she told me I wasn't playing with the gifts God gave me. She told me I wasn't working hard, that I thought I was a big man now and I could do what I wanted instead of paying attention to the game. She doesn't just know me as a person; she knows baseball and could tell me what she was seeing as wrong. I had to stop and listen to her, to see it through her eyes that I had to focus better. I didn't want to hear it from my coach, my manager, reporters, my teammates, or the fans, but from my mother? I knew I needed to listen to her."

A change of attitude and lots of spring workouts with a catching coach, and Benito was feeling more like the player his mother reminded him he should be. On the offensive side, he slammed in his one hundredth home run in May, becoming only the fifth catcher to do so.

"When you're young, you feel so good when you get a home run or hit well and that just doesn't matter. Like I said before, in my first few years, I didn't understand this. Winning is what matters, not whatever an individual player wants that day. No, I didn't like going 0-4, but if we win, that counts more than if I go 4-4 and we lose.

"In my fourth year going into the fifth in the majors was around when I really learned why thinking about what pitch to call is so important—especially if you're behind late in the game. You don't get extra points for being ahead in the beginning of the game. Late in the innings—seventh to the ninth is when you win or lose. The manager and I played the game like I was a manager—I developed a good sense for this. Everything is about helping the pitcher win. Look, at the end of the game, the pitcher is usually the one who gets interviewed, not the catcher. The thing is, though, all pitchers think they're smart, but they always want to throw a fast ball and it takes more than that. They think if they throw 100 or 101 miles per hour, it will get past the hitter. It's impressive, but the velocity isn't the main point. Good hitters train for fast balls, so where a pitcher puts the ball is what makes the difference.

"As the catcher, I had to connect with the pitcher, but still be in command of the game. I worked very hard on knowing if a hitter can hit and concentrated on remembering them from inning to inning. I had to manage the pitchers as they swapped out. The other pitchers are in the dugout, and they probably aren't watching the game—they're talking about whatever, what they're doing that night, etc. I'm the one who has been paying attention to what's been going on. That's why I have to control the pitcher, and I can't focus on just one pitcher—it has to be the pitchers combined. It's the total ERA that counts, and as the catcher, I can't care about just what one of them does. Sure, each pitcher wants his stats to be as good as they can, but it's the team that goes to the play-offs or not. An individual pitcher makes the All-Stars and that's good for him, just like it was good for me to be selected. That's not what wins games though. As a professional, getting at least into the play-offs is what everyone's goal should be.

"The manager often talked to me first about whether to pull a pitcher, but we would do that before the inning started, not during. I could go to the manager and suggest it and it would happen sometimes, and, yeah, the pitcher would almost always get mad. I understood why, but I had to tell the truth from what I was seeing at my angle. This is why catchers make good managers—you've been doing some of the same things if you're a good catcher. I remember about how managers told me, if we're winning after the seventh inning—if the hitter is right-handed, make him hit to the left and vice versa. I didn't believe it made a difference and learned they were correct. It gives you a better chance of controlling the hitter. You also have to know when to go inside or outside, and the pitcher isn't thinking about all these things. There were pitchers who understood the relationship and would ask for me not to have a day off if they were pitching. That's the kind of relationship you want to develop and is the best combination for a pitcher and catcher.

"The decision to walk a player is another thing. It's the manager's call, but if you've got somebody up who's an All-Star, you have to look to see who's behind him. Even if that guy has been hitting better than usual, you know he isn't as consistent, and it's probably smarter taking a chance with him. With me being a veteran when I came to Miami, I was able to help with younger players now that I understood the game better. I explained how they had to take care of themselves, play smart, and always be ready. You can't let your guard down if you're ahead, and you don't have to be too discouraged if you're behind early on. You don't believe it when you're first playing, but you do learn a lot of games turn in the last two innings."

With Benito's renewed level of play, it's difficult to know how the full second year in Miami would have actually turned out. By the end of the first half of the season, the Miami Marlins were at forty-one wins and forty-seven losses. Although being ahead at that point was preferred, they weren't in a bad situation. What neither Benito nor the other players could see approaching in the weeks to come was the professional baseball strike of 1994, which brought the season to a standstill.

Baseball is a multibillion-dollar business, and with that kind of money at stake, there are many factors involved and no shortage of opinions when owners and players clash over salary and revenues. There are several books and hundreds (if not thousands) of articles on what led up to the strike and the lasting impact on baseball. To greatly simplify complicated pieces of the puzzle, the 1990 Collective Bargaining Agreement between owners and the players' union was due to expire December 31, 1994. With free agency firmly fixed in the sport, owners wanted some sort of salary cap in whatever new agreement was reached. The union wouldn't hear of it, and the hard line was drawn. There had been seven previous work stoppages since 1972 with the duration from as few as two days to as long as fifty days.

This time, both sides underestimated the resolve of their opposing views, and when August 12, 1994, dawned, it was to silent stadiums and plenty of angry people. Since the World Series was first played in 1903, it had been cancelled only in 1904—not even World War I or World War II had caused a halt. The same could not be said for the 1994 strike.

"We never imagined we wouldn't be able to finish the season or have a post-season," Benito grimaced. "We didn't know what was going to happen next. The players didn't want the strike, the fans didn't, and I lost at least a million dollars because of the strike, maybe more. It was terrible for the sport."

Benito was financially able to sit out the strike and refused to join replacement players in a short-lived effort by the owners to force the union to come to a settlement. Millions of dollars were lost across a wide swath of the economy all the way down to the guys who sold peanuts in the stands. Montreal arguably suffered the greatest impact as the Expos team was relocated to ultimately become the Washington Nationals [Washington, D.C.]. With rumors rampant that the 1995 season might be in danger, more than one talented veteran verging on breaking records chose to retire instead of waiting to see what might happen. For many sports fans, there was a lingering "what-if" question as notable names disappeared from rosters. Michael Jordan, the famous Chicago Bulls basketball icon, ready for spring training with the White Sox, returned to basketball instead, never playing a single major league game.

With the strike stretching through the winter months and anxieties building about 1995, an unanticipated "first" in Major League history emerged. And it happened in Homestead, Florida, which is located midway between south Miami and Key Largo. The Florida Turnpike ends at the intersection of Highway 1 and Palm Drive. Going straight puts you on the Overseas Highway that literally ends in Key West. A right-hand turn takes you toward the famous Everglades National Park. A left-hand turn leads past the Homestead Sports Complex. Baseball history buffs might know Homestead briefly as a "Baseball City" in the 1960s. The St. Louis Cardinals Minor League set up their winter headquarters for a while there, and both Stan Musial and Roberto Clemente were among players who thrilled fans in games at different times. Still considered a bit out-of-the-way by most teams for Grapefruit League spring training, the city had its hopes raised in discussions with the Cleveland Indians. Homestead built a baseball stadium in 1991 as the main part of the complex, never imagining the extraordinary destruction of Hurricane Andrew of 1992 as a possibility. The area and layout of the complex did allow it to become a command center for hurricane relief efforts, yet when rebuilding was over, so was any pending deal with Cleveland. An array of Major League players and coaches did arrive, however, in April 1995 as the Major League Baseball Players Association put together a special spring training camp for more than two dozen free agents who weren't yet signed.

This was hardly the type of spring training Benito was looking for, and the mood was not the usual back-slapping reunion. The arrangement did provide a chance for the players to work out, however, and occasional jokes were made about maybe they could simply create their own team. The attractive contracts Benito had finally been able to command weren't feasible given the circumstances. The new season was looming, and he was one of the last holdouts. "A lot of teams were able to sign players they could never have afforded if it hadn't been for the strike. I went to Cincinnati for much less money than I would have, but you do what's necessary in situations like that and make the best of it."

Benito, who had literally cried for joy when Pete Rose had his record-breaking 4,256th hit and been stunned when the legend's career was ruined by scandal, would now put on the uniform of the same team as one of his childhood baseball heroes.

Chapter Seven
Other Teams, Other Cities

"Davey Johnson was the manager in Cincinnati. I also think of him as one of my best managers—I was lucky to have a lot of good ones. I saw him a few years ago in Washington, and we talked and I was able to say thank you for things I didn't really understand when I was there. It was a little tough for all of us in Cincinnati because the fans weren't coming at first—you can understand they were still upset about the strike."

Winning the fans back after the prolonged and painful strike was not going to be easy, and as attendance figures limped along, the Cincinnati Reds couldn't count their opening games as encouraging. As they say in every sport, though, "How you start the season isn't what matters." The Reds put a string of early losses behind them, and talk of post-season play became more than wishful thinking. A July game with a 10-1 win over the Chicago Cubs and Benito getting two home runs were setting the stage. Emotions at times did spark, such as at the September 6 game with the Houston Astros when eight players were ejected after a series of confrontations, one of which started when Benito was bumped after he scored a run.

"I don't remember getting into a brawl that time specifically. But look, we're all professionals, and I don't start things with a team we're playing. Sometimes, it's like getting bumped, and other times it starts because a pitcher deliberately hits a guy. I'm behind the plate watching, and you can always tell by a pitcher's eyes if it's deliberate.

They know they shouldn't do it, but if the other team's pitcher hits one of our guys on purpose, you better expect us to do something in return. That's the way the game works and, yeah, things can get out of control."

Cincinnati, as one of the five teams realigned in 1994 to create the National League Central, had an 85-59 record to put them up against the Los Angeles Dodgers in the National League Division Series. The Reds won the Division, but ended up losing the National League Championship to the Atlanta Braves, who went on to win the World Series that year.

Making it to the post-season, eleven home runs, forty-four RBIs, and leading the National League catchers with a .996 fielding percentage put Benito in a position for bargaining, and Cincinnati wasn't going to keep him without a better offer. Philadelphia, whose catcher wasn't fully recovered from surgery, didn't mind writing a contract for $1.1 million plus incentives. It was time to try out the City of Brotherly Love.

"I don't regret having been in Cincinnati. They made their business decision, and I made mine. I was playing the way I liked, but if I have to pick the best thing that happened to me, it was meeting Johnny Bench. To have him come sit down and talk to me was very lucky, and I had fun with him. He told me I was a good player and talked about how important it was for me to take care of myself. I mean, here is the guy I used to watch on TV. I don't care what age you are, you get to meet one of your heroes and it's like you're ten years old again. The funny part is, for me now, I go to a game and I want to talk to the catcher. It was the same thing Johnny Bench and those guys did for me, and I find myself doing it. That's the difference when you're older—you see how you can maybe help. When you're young, you're playing and you think you know everything, but you don't."

The move to Philadelphia could have been a good match—Benito had a strong year, setting an offensive team record for catchers by batting in 136 games with seventy-one runs, twenty-one doubles, two triples, and thirty home runs. "I don't know what it was about Veteran's Stadium [in Philadelphia], but I loved hitting in that ballpark. I still can't figure out why that year was so much better for home runs. I didn't do anything special, and I told everyone not to get used to it. I could usually expect to get fifteen or so home runs in regular season, and I was as surprised as anyone with getting thirty that year."

Of all the home runs, two games early in the season were the most memorable. "This was a pitcher I knew pretty well," he said of the cold April day after they'd beaten Pittsburgh in the first of the two-game series. "He threw a sinker, and I was waiting for him." That homer brought in three runners for Philadelphia to regain the lead and go on to sweep the series.

Less than a month later, though, was the kind of play fans talk about around the proverbial water cooler when they say, *Yeah, I was there and saw it. It was great!* Greg Maddux was on the mound in Atlanta, and the Braves pitcher was an undisputed star. Benito had been justifiably glad to score a home run off him in the fifth inning, and it was the ninth with the bases loaded. They were loaded because Maddux had intentionally walked the previous batter. "Look, like I said, the manager is the one who makes the decision to walk a hitter and, okay, he's thinking I'm not going to get a second hit. Sure, I was a free swinger and I had a lot of respect for Maddux, but knowing they were thinking that made me determined to really focus and be ready for whatever he threw. One of the things I learned was I often performed better if there was someone on base. I don't know why, maybe the extra pressure made me better; maybe there really wasn't a difference. I wanted this one bad though—to get at least a single and bring a runner in. More than that would be good."

It was spectacularly *more* and *good*. In over a decade of his pitching career, no player had ever hit a grand slam off Maddux. When Benito rocketed the ball out of the park, Maddux could no longer claim that distinction. Those high moments weren't enough, however, to take Philadelphia above fifth place in the National League.

"I don't know why Philly didn't sign me again," Benito shrugged. "You don't let it get to you, though; you make another deal. I was a strong player, and a team signs me as the catcher, I'm their guy. I don't sit out for many games; the back-up catcher isn't going to have a chance to play unless I get hurt. That was something you could depend on and didn't change no matter what team I played for. I kept myself in shape and Philly didn't want me to stay, that was okay. I had plenty of years left in me. You're a free agent and you move on."

The Toronto Blue Jays felt the same way. In leaving the historic Phillies, established in 1883, Benito was going to another expansion team. Toronto's inaugural season was 1976. By 1985, they'd captured their first American League East Division title. They began setting attendance records, and in 1989, Toronto showed the world the SkyDome, an enclosed multiuse stadium with a fully retractable motorized roof—the first time this feature was incorporated into a sports stadium. It drew worldwide attention, a venue to be proud of. What could be even better? Win your second division title three months later. There was more to follow, though, and in 1992, the ultimate goal was achieved as Toronto not only reached, but won the World Series. Can you do that twice? Not easily. When deliriously happy fans cheered the 1993 victory, it was only the fourteenth occurrence of back-to-back series wins in the history of the World Series. The Toronto Blue Jays joined a list of champions that included the New York Giants, Chicago Cubs, Philadelphia Athletics, Boston Red Sox, New York Yankees, Oakland A's, and the Cincinnati Reds.

Fans hunger for continued glory even when they know the odds are against any team to have multiple sequential wins. Still, the next season brought some disappointment along with what had been some cost-cutting measures. Although Toronto did finish 1996 with a better record than 1995, rebuilding the team became a priority. The type of players Toronto wanted were no longer coming off the rebound of the 1994 strike, but if you're going to bring in pitcher Roger Clemens from the Boston Red Sox, having Benito behind the plate was a valuable combination.

"I knew him [Clemens] before we played together. As a catcher, it's best to learn as much as you can about a lot of different pitchers because you never know when you might be on a team together. Roger Clemens was one of those pitchers who has a lot of power with his arm and used his mind. I say all the time that a pitcher can throw a ball one hundred miles per hour and he thinks he owns the stadium, and that's the wrong way to think. Clemens wasn't like that, and it was an honor to catch for him. He was one of the best pitchers during my era, as he was only a few years older than me. He took the game to another level because of the way that he prepared for the games and the way that he pitched. He was about power, and he was a power pitcher. Not all big guys—he was taller than me and not skinny like I was—can control their power like he could. He taught me how to be with other pitchers, too. He understood that the catcher was number one for controlling the game. I played with him for just one year and then he won the Cy Young, which is a huge award for anyone. One of the things I learned from him was about when the catcher should go to the mound to talk to the pitcher and how to work with future pitchers. It wasn't like I was a rookie at that point, but he would talk to me in a way that helped me understand how a pitcher might be thinking. From almost the very beginning, we shared the calls on the pitches and had a good rapport. He trusted my calls, but we really worked well together understanding what pitch was needed. I learned a lot from him that I used for the rest of my career."

The season did see Clemens as the Cy Young winner and with attendance at more than 2.5 million the team came in fifth in the American League East.

"I can't say I had ever thought about playing for Toronto, but they love baseball there and they do have a great stadium. Clean, my God, the city is so clean you have to wonder if they have that many people working on it all the time or maybe people are more careful. You go to all the big cities when you're in baseball—Chicago, Atlanta, Los Angeles, New York—and you're not going to find clean like Toronto." There was an unexpected down side to the attractive $4 million contract, however. "What nobody told me about was the taxes. It was crazy what I was paying. If I had understood before how much it was going to cost me in taxes, I'm not so sure I would have signed with them. These are all the things you have to learn and ask questions about. I had been around long enough I probably should have thought about it, but that one got by me."

Despite the beauty of the city, Toronto winters were hardly something Benito wanted to endure, especially not with owning a house in South Florida. And what's a house in Florida without a boat to enjoy and a Ferrari as part of your luxury car collection? Although Benito didn't let himself go physically during the off-season, he set aside leisure time to relax and unwind. He could take a break from the possibility of getting injured during a game where 100-plus-miles-an-hour balls were hurtled his way and runners were prepared to knock him down to reach home plate. No, the months between season's end and spring training weren't usually anything to worry about since Benito wasn't into extreme sports or hobbies. He was looking forward to what should have been a laid-back, normal day in January 1998, until it took a terrible and unexpected turn.

Chapter Eight
A Mangled Body

"My house in Fort Lauderdale had a dock behind it where I kept my boat, and a friend from Puerto Rico was the mechanic who worked on it if it didn't need to go into the marina. He came over to do some work and had to stop to go to the store to pick up a part." Benito paused for a moment remembering what, at the time, was an inconsequential exchange. "It was one of those things you don't think about. I had the Ferrari there—this one was a yellow convertible. I didn't drive it all that often, but my friend had never been in one. He was going to take his truck and said he'd really enjoy a ride in the Ferrari if I didn't mind. I wasn't busy and it wouldn't take long, so I told him to get in. My son was staying with me, and I put him in the car, too, but then another friend who was staying came out and saw us. There were only two seats, and I had put my son in the middle between us. My friend took a look and said something like, 'Come on, Benny, there's no real room in the car for the kid. Let him stay here with me.' Thanks to God he did that because I don't think there is any way he [the son] could have survived.

"I wanted to show my mechanic friend how smoothly the car accelerated, and I had the green light at this intersection. I shot through it and didn't see right away another car wasn't stopping on red. When I realized he was running the light, I cut the wheel sharply to avoid him. I hit the sidewalk before the car bounced off that and slammed into a tree. It's hard to describe how fast everything happened. I was trying to figure out how bad things were and felt a little panic because at first I couldn't feel my legs. The passenger seat was empty, and I didn't know where my friend was. My face was wet all over, something blurring my eyes. I looked over, and there was this guy standing on the sidewalk who must have seen the whole thing. He was staring, and I asked him for his shirt so I could wipe my face, but he didn't come close. I was thinking I must look really terrible. It probably wasn't long before I could finally move, and I realized the driver's door was gone, too. It had launched through the windshield, and I was covered in broken glass. As I managed to crawl out, I saw the bushes were moving. I'm having weird thoughts like maybe it's a dog or something, but it's my friend dragging himself toward me. His leg was horrible. He asked how it was, and I saw he had no skin all the way to his ankle. I told him not to look. We were both losing a lot of blood. I passed out before the police and ambulance arrived. It might have looked to them like I was dead. Or maybe not—I guess they see a lot of awful wrecks."

Benito and his passenger were rushed to the nearest hospital in Fort Lauderdale. "I woke up in the trauma center. I could hear my friend screaming in pain. I thought I was going to pass out again, but they were trying to keep me awake to see how bad the head injury was. A lot of the blood had come from a bunch of cuts to my face and head and, for sure, I had a concussion. They entered me into the hospital under a false name because they needed to get me past the trauma stage and into a room before the press and other people came looking to talk to me. It didn't take long to make the news.

"Something I wasn't expecting was they had film footage of the wreckage they kept showing on TV like every hour for a couple of days. The entire back of the car was demolished, and if I hadn't hit the sidewalk before the tree, my friend would have been thrown directly into the tree. He must have not had his seatbelt on. I don't really remember. I couldn't help watching it over and over, thanking God I was alive, and mostly thanking God my other friend had talked me into leaving my son at the house. There were times when I wondered if it wouldn't have been less damage if I had hit the car that ran the light instead of trying to avoid him. You can never know about that kind of thing—maybe it would have been worse and that driver hurt badly."

In the waning days of the Christmas and New Year's holiday, there was a Christmas tree atop a large building outside Benito's hospital room. He watched it lit up at night and worried about his condition and his future. "I had four different doctors, and I'm thinking I must be really bad to need four."

Once the tests revealed no lasting brain trauma, the doctors predicted the concussion and lacerations would heal easily, although the scarring would be permanent. The fractured vertebra, broken pelvis, and ligament damage to his right knee—those were the injuries the doctors said would do more than end his career. "They told me I might never walk right again, that it would take four or five years to recuperate, and there was no way I could return to baseball. I was in pain, so much pain; I can't tell you how bad it was, but I told them they had to be wrong. I wasn't going to accept that; I was going to find a way to show they were wrong. I was in the hospital for a month, and my mom came to be with me.

"Being in bed unable to get up, I didn't understand how bad the lower part of my body was. The doctor finally said I could try to go to the bathroom on my own, and my knee immediately collapsed on me. I was mad with everyone and then apologized. They said they understood. I was crying like a child at times when I thought maybe the doctors were correct and I had to give up baseball. I was on morphine, and I was scared. Even with the morphine, it got to where I couldn't sleep worrying that I wouldn't recover. The thought of not recovering was almost harder than the pain. My brain was constantly spinning around, and I kept thinking that I was going to go home and be nobody without baseball in my life. I was going to be one more player whose career was cut short by injury, by an accident that probably shouldn't have happened."

There are out-and-out miracles when it comes to medical injuries; then there is the combination of advanced technology, skilled care, and individual determination. The only good thing about the wreck, which occurred on January 4, 1998, was it gave Benito a few months before the start of spring training. An experienced physical therapist came to him, a man who had seen him play and who shared Benito's belief that it wasn't right for his career to end this way. "He said he wanted to see me play again, to see me throw from my knees. He said it would be hard, but they could help me."

"They" were the staff at Health South, a major presence in the world of physical rehabilitation with multiple locations in Florida. [The facility where Benito was treated was later closed and a new one opened not far away.]

"I can't believe I've forgotten their names. I thought for sure I would remember them forever for what they did for me. I feel bad I can't remember."

As Health South describes on its website (www.healthsouth.com), it takes a unique approach to rehabilitation. Its superbly trained physicians and therapists work closely together with the understanding that no matter what elements may be common among patients, there is no "one-size-fits-all solution." The facility has an impressive list of success stories of individuals who have recovered from severe conditions.

Benito's in-patient stay wasn't long. The first part of the process was a thorough evaluation to assess the correct approach to take for his recovery and to develop a customized plan to allow him to be treated predominantly in an out-patient capacity. "The progress was really slow at first, and I was in pain all the time. I accused people of lying to me about how I was doing, then I felt terrible for what I said and apologized. I'm thinking: Okay, what am I going to do now? Baseball is my life, I haven't been to college—it will be all over for me. Then one day, everything switched. I decided, no, I am going to be motivated to play again. So, this guy who was working most with me, who had told me he wanted to see me play again, took me to a stairway and we looked to the top. There were at least seven or maybe as many as ten flights up. He told me that when I could make it all the way up there without help, that would mean I was back to where I could walk right. If I could walk right, I could find a way to get back in shape to play baseball. I gave it a try, and I couldn't get past the first step. What did that mean? The guy said, 'I'll help you with the first few steps, then it's up to you.' I was praying to God every morning from then on, and it was like he was talking back to me saying, 'You got to work hard, kid.' There was a lot of up and down for the next few weeks. At one point, I thought there was no way this was going to work and I should give up. I kept trying all the exercises, though, and going to those stairs, and I started to see improvement. Even only a few steps was a sign to me."

The effort was grueling. "I thanks God for these people. There were days when I hurt so much that I was nasty to them. I knew it wasn't their fault and I shouldn't curse and be angry. They were helping me, and every time it happened, I told myself not to be that way, not to take everything out on them. They were great, though, and told me it was okay, they understood why I was reacting in a bad way. How they did what they did, I don't know. And my mom Nelida. My mom, she was there with me the whole time, taking me to therapy, telling me I could do this. Those stairs, they were the way to show me I was getting better. The guy was right. The pain never really went away, but I got to where I could handle it, and on the day I climbed to the top, I was crying in happiness more than with the pain."

The doctors who treated and diagnosed Benito were competent doctors, well qualified in their expertise. Their collective belief that he couldn't return to baseball was a logical conclusion, and for all the good the team of Health South did for him, they couldn't repair the damage to his knee.

Among the many specialties in the world of medicine, there is the field of sports medicine. Doctors in this field understand that the demands placed on athletes' bodies are different from what a normal person requires. For baseball players, rotator cuff tears and the less publicized torn labrum [cuff of cartilage surrounding the shoulder joint socket], severe elbow inflammation, and arthritis are especially seen in pitchers. Hands and wrists are more vulnerable than often realized, particularly the small wrist bone, the hamate, which is prone to fracture. Knee injuries of torn meniscus and anterior cruciate ligament (ACL) aren't confined to football or basketball. Concussions and torn muscles can be the result of collisions. When Tony Conigliaro took a ball to the cheekbone in 1946, the break healed and he returned to baseball, but the associated damage to his eye ultimately ended his career. No matter the source of the injury—be it on the field or off, as in the case with Benito, the performance level to which a professional athlete has to return is generally higher than for someone who is moderately active.

One of the doctors with a stellar reputation and known across the sports spectrum was Doctor James Andrews, of the Andrews Sports Medicine and Orthopedic Center in Birmingham, Alabama.

"Dr. Andrews, he's a genius. He's who everybody goes to. He's the man who can tell you if you have a chance to make it back to the game. He can't do it for you, but if he says it's possible, then you have to decide what to do for yourself."

Benito traveled to Alabama, uncertain of what the outcome would be. He was filled with hope that the new prognosis would be more positive than the original. He was accepted as a patient, and the surgery was successful. The physical therapy that followed was just as important as the first rounds had been.

"It was hard, but nothing had changed in my mind since I was released from the hospital. My whole life had been baseball, and there was nothing else I wanted to do. Much later when things were better, the guy who had helped me so much with my therapy came to one of my games. I still can't believe I have forgotten his name. I found out he was there in the stands. I told him to come with me to the clubhouse. He didn't think he should and said he just wanted the chance to see me play the way we had talked about. I hugged him and brought him out of his seat and brought him in with the players. I wanted to do a hundred things for him all at the same time. Dr. Andrews, he was a great guy and an amazing surgeon, but the operation couldn't restore all the strength I had lost. That had to come with therapy, and I told the guy who helped me climb those stairs I understood he was the reason I could play again. I hope to see him again someday. Maybe he'll read this book and get in touch with me. I'll take him out to dinner, and we'll talk about everything he did for me."

Toronto kept Benito on its active roster, and as part of his physical rehabilitation cycle, he was sent to Texas to work with the club's minor league team. Playing there would help management gauge the pace of Benito's recovery, and he could give advice to the younger players. Mike Rodriguez, born in the Dominican Republic and raised in New York, had avidly watched Benito on television when he was growing up. "It was terrible he got hurt as badly as he did," Mike recalled, "but for me to get to play with him in the minors—I was in awe. He became my mentor, and it wasn't only me. He went out of his way to help all the Latin players. He gave advice and took them out to nice restaurants to have lobster and teach them how to act. Most, like him, came from incredibly poor backgrounds, and when he talked, it was coming from someone who genuinely understood how awkward it can be and how they didn't want to ask certain questions because they didn't want to sound stupid. They understood he had been where they were and he was telling them things they needed to know. When you're poor in the islands, you don't have many options, and for those kids who couldn't get out any other way, baseball was about their only opportunity. To have Benito Santiago there with them was a real inspiration. They were pretty nervous being around him, and so for a while, I acted kind of like a go-between. The other part for me personally is I had never imagined having Benito Santiago giving me pointers about being a catcher. It was some of the best training I could have asked for."

Benito was to have only fifteen games with the Blue Jays late that year, and it didn't come as a surprise when they didn't sign him for a third season. "I was able to play, but I wasn't fully recovered. It wasn't me playing like I had been or planned to be able to again. I couldn't blame them for not wanting to take the chance I might not make it. A lot of people in the sport were convinced I was wasting my time. I was going to use off-season to do everything I could and get stronger. I didn't know what team I would be with, but God didn't kill me in the wreck when he could have, and I had been through too much to accept the idea my career was over. I had years of playing left in me, and at that point, it didn't matter who I went with—it was being on a team again to show the world Benito Santiago wasn't finished yet."

Even though Benito no longer left a ticket at his home games in the name of his birth father, Jose, he'd felt his presence every time he stepped onto a ball field. He knew the spirit of the man whose image was tattooed on his arm wanted to see him behind the plate for a while longer.

Chapter Nine
Proving the Experts Wrong

"It's funny in a way, but one of the first things I did when I decided I was going to find a way to get back to baseball was go out and buy another Ferrari. My mom, oh, was she mad at me. 'You're being stupid,' she said, and I told her, 'No, Mom, that car was a convertible and this one has a hard top.' She didn't like me making the joke, but didn't say anything else to me about it.

"One of the most important things outside the rehab was taking up on the offer made to me by Paul Casanova. He's Cuban, another Latin catcher who made the All-Stars, and was a hero to us when we were watching baseball as kids. He had a batting cage and a pitching machine at his house, and he told me to come there for special workouts. It made a big difference being able to do that, especially with someone like him who understood how a catcher has to move. He was even built kind of like me, tall and thin when he was playing. He could be a good judge of my progress—see things in the way that mattered in playing baseball."

The Chicago Cubs were willingly to believe Benito had worked hard at recovery, and after having him thoroughly checked by their own medical team and watching him at spring training, the Cubs signed Benito to play the 1999 season on the famous Wrigley Field, where the team had been playing since 1916.

The 1999 Cubs roster included Sammy Sosa, a name that had been constantly in the news the prior year. "You know who helped the most in getting baseball back on track after the strike? Sammy Sosa and Mark McGwire. Fans weren't coming to the games like they had been before the strike. All the teams were faced with the same problem, and it got better quicker in some cities than in others. The home run battle between Sosa and McGwire was really something, and it was what the fans needed to see. The excitement of these guys coming up to bat and everyone wondering how long the streak could last and who was going to come out on top—it made people care about baseball again. It wasn't just fans caught up—lots of other people knew about the competition, too. People who didn't usually talk about baseball were following it in the news. Nobody I played with had ever seen anything like it."

That had been the previous season when baseball news had been dominated by Sosa with the Chicago Cubs and McGwire with the St. Louis Cardinals as they both chased the record New York Yankee Roger Maris had set in 1961 with sixty-one home runs in a single season. McGwire reached the goal first on September 8, 1998, rather ironically as the Cardinals were playing the Cubs. Sosa was still hanging at fifty-eight home runs, but tied McGwire less than two weeks later at sixty-three. When the final count ended, McGwire had seventy to Sosa's sixty-six home runs, and the anticipated $1 million auction for the baseball McGwire scored with soared all the way to $3 million.

Although the fans didn't actually believe there would be a repeat home-run battle in 1999, the excitement lingered. Wrigley Field saw more than 2.8 million attendees during the season, and Benito was there with Sammy Sosa and others as starters on Opening Day. "I think Sosa got sixty-three home runs that year, only three less than the year before. He and I had a lot of respect for each other as players on the field."

For Benito, it was a mixed time, balancing the determination to play with the reality of residual pain. "My body is something special, part of who I am, being tall and skinny with long fingers. I still had my strong throwing arm and the knee had been repaired as well as it could be, but I wasn't where I wanted to be physically. I couldn't move the way I used to yet. I didn't want to admit how much it hurt some days, and if the doctor could have seen me to examine me, he probably would have told me I was trying too hard. For me, it was important to play every game as hard as I could. That was the Benito Santiago I had been for my whole career—why wouldn't it be the same for me now?"

In thinking of his age and recovery, it brought to mind one of those encounters he hadn't thought about for several years. "I was at spring training and getting ready to go into the batting cage. This really old guy was standing around—you get all kinds of people who come to spring training for different reasons, and you don't really pay attention to them unless someone introduces you. I can tell this guy is watching me, and he says something like, 'You're pretty old to be doing this, aren't you? You planning to play much longer?' I don't remember exactly what I said to him, but I'm thinking to myself about who this guy is he talks to me like this. Is he trying to disrespect me? Why should he? What does he know anyway? I finish up in the cage, and I'm talking to one of the other players, and I tell him what happened, and I'm a little mad by now thinking about it. He looks at me and says, 'You don't know who that is?' I tell him no and he starts laughing. 'That's Yogi Berra.' Oh man, now I'm worried about what I said to him. Was *I* disrespectful? So I went over and I said, 'Mr. Berra, I didn't realize it was you. I'm sorry if I said something I shouldn't have.' He was good, though, and we talked for a little bit after that.

"You have to be careful like that because you don't ever know for sure who might be around a ball club. The thing with your sports heroes is you have a habit of only seeing them in your head at their peak. Actors and other celebrities, they can be in the movies or on TV playing older characters and you get used to them having white hair and wrinkles. Athletes, though, unless they get on TV as commentators, you don't see them the same way. I'm fifty-two now. Some kid who is maybe fifteen won't have watched me play, but he has an early baseball card with my picture, and it won't look like I do. You put a rookie card of me next to a photo of me now when I'm not in a baseball uniform and I can't blame a young player for not knowing it's me. It's the name people remember in sports, not as much the face."

Benito was behind the plate for more than 66 percent of the games with the Cubs and managed seven home runs and thirty-six RBIs; his strength lagging behind what he wanted despite working through the pain. His first team back might not have been a good fit no matter which it had been, and Benito's parting from the Cubs was through mutual agreement.

His old coach Jack McKeon was in Cincinnati, and he probably understood Benito's abilities and his intensity about playing as well as anyone in baseball. The Reds' 1999 season may have ended with a wild-card loss to stop their playoff chances, but McKeon had been named as National League Manager of the Year and signing Ken Griffey Jr. created a buzz. Like McKeon, there were fans who remembered Benito from his first time in Cincinnati and hopes were high for what the 2000 season would bring. For Benito, it was a chance to work with a man he felt a strong bond to and a team and city he was familiar with. In only their seventh game, he dislocated a knuckle in his left hand and was out for almost two weeks—not the kind of start he had intended. His first game back after the mild injury, though, had the home crowd cheering. His catching showed off his old zing, and he brought in another runner with a home run.

Even though the team did enjoy more wins than losses, post-season eluded them, and it was made more disappointing by the early predictions of how great the year was anticipated to be. Every manager in every professional sport can attest to the fact that the environment in the manager's office can be as tough as on the playing field. With eighty-five games in the win column and coming in second place in the Central Division, McKeon's contract was not renewed.

Unlike in Chicago, the number of games Benito's played dropped to 54 percent although he was sixth on the roster for RBIs. For him, however, the next move was one he was genuinely looking forward to. The Giant's manager, Dusty Baker, was a man he admired and his call came at the right time before spring training was to commence. Paul Casanova, the man with the batting cage at his house, was friends with Dusty Baker and set the deal into motion.

"Paul called and told me Benito had been working out with him and he was ready," Dusty remembers. "Paul and I were with the Braves together—he actually threw some from his knees, too. I'd watched Benito for years. What an exciting rookie he was. After I became a manager, I'd thought about him, but he wasn't available at certain times and I couldn't afford him. Or at least I was told I couldn't. So, the chance for him comes up and it was a tough choice. I had to go with him or Doug Mirabelli. Age would have been a factor for another catcher, but Benito was Benito. He stayed lean and agile, didn't let his weight get away from him."

In closing the deal, though, the man who had done so much for Benito for most of his career was no longer at his side. "One of the biggest mistakes I ever made was letting Scott Boras go as my agent. He did so much for me, but this is what happens. You get to be big, and you think it's all you. You're the one out there playing, and you can always find another agent, find another team. You don't want to listen to good advice. This is how your mind can start to work, and you can't see it in the right way until later after things are over. You're convinced it will last forever. What I did to Scott wasn't right. I hope to see him again someday, and that way I can tell him I'm sorry man-to-man."

Although their original roots were in the baseball-loving New York City, the Giants were in their fifth decade in San Francisco and Benito was certain he would finally be back in full form. "I wasn't signed to be the starting catcher, and Dusty Baker said he couldn't make a promise about how many games I would play. I didn't mind because I knew I had to show him I was back for real. He had a reputation for understanding players can be injured or have some kind of problem affecting their play and need longer than a season to recover. He wouldn't know for sure until after he saw me in action. He was giving me a chance, and that was the most important thing then. I felt very positive I was ready, but I wouldn't know either until the season started."

Chapter Ten
Home of the Giants

The historic moves of the Brooklyn Dodgers to Los Angeles and the New York Giants to San Francisco in the late 1950s happened almost a decade before Benito was born. Being part of a team with a history that dates to the beginning of baseball has a certain allure. Being part of an expansion team, especially in its first year like with the Marlins, brings a different perspective. Teams that relocate fall into another category as fans and cities "left behind" might feel betrayed or say "good riddance" instead, depending on how acrimonious the negotiations became. The city receiving a MLB franchise is generally wildly enthusiastic, or it wouldn't have expended the effort and resources to court a team. Of the current thirty MLB teams, five have moved once, two have moved twice, and two have made three relocations. There have been a number of team name changes that didn't always equate to physical moves, and, of course, many teams have built new, bigger, sometimes jaw-dropping stadiums. In more than one case, the agreement for a new stadium has been clinched in order to keep a team in place or attract one.

In Benito's time as a catcher, he experienced playing for teams in each of these categories. No matter the city, though, the common denominator for Benito was his love of baseball and his love for the fans. What he didn't know on the day he signed with San Francisco in 2001 was that he had landed on a team that would bring him to a goal he had almost given up on.

The lingering scars that left visible signs from his accident had never been a matter of concern to him. After all, he had always had somewhat of a tough guy swagger. The scars were testament of survival and a reminder of how close he had come to literal death and figurative death from a career point of view. He was equally grateful that the hidden pain he'd been dealing with for two seasons had become easier to manage. As remarkable as his comeback from his injuries had been, considering the bleak January 1998 assessment when doctors doubted he would walk again without at least the need of a cane, the normal physical stress on a catcher was something Benito was realistic about. Very much a veteran player at age thirty-six, he weighed only ten pounds more than when he was in the minors.

"For me, I know what happens to catchers who let their upper bodies get bigger. It's tougher on your knees, and your knees go as a catcher, it's almost as bad as if your arm does. The surgery and physical therapy to repair my knee wouldn't have helped much if I had put on a lot of weight. I hadn't been playing the high number of games I was used to and that meant I had to pay attention to other workouts. I wasn't going to let anybody be able to say I wasn't doing everything I could to be in the right shape. Just being in San Francisco felt good from the beginning, better than since I had the wreck. God gave me a special talent and a body built for baseball. When I was in the hospital trying to recover, I kept praying to have the chance to play like myself before. Being with the Giants was how I was going to do that."

The team where he would get the opportunity he was seeking was positioned well going into the 2001 season. They had inaugurated their new Pacific Bell Park, and setting aside some early losses, they won their second National League West title in four years with a 97-65 record. They didn't make it past the New York Mets to win the National League Championship, but more than 3 million fans had attended the home games and Dusty Baker was named Manager of the Year.

Benito, confident he would move up to starter after a few games, didn't enter the new clubhouse with his old degree of cockiness; that had mellowed some during the process of everything he'd been through. What he wasn't expecting was to immediately meet two of the other Hall of Fame heroes he'd admired since he was a kid. "The first guys I saw in the clubhouse were Willie Mays, Willie McCovey, and a pitcher. After that, I sat with them almost every day. I didn't know Willie Mays personally before then because I came into the game a while after him, but what a guy to talk to. He had a big influence on my game like some of the other greats I've talked about. One time a trainer named Murph asked Willie Mays, 'If Benito is behind the plate, do you think he will get you out?' And Willie Mays said, 'Benito would have to throw the ball to third base because if he threw the ball to second he would have no chance because I was so fast.' That was funny and he might have been right. Willie talked to me a lot, and he had great stories."

If there were still skeptics in the press and the stands who thought Benito was too old and wouldn't be seen often behind the plate, he didn't mind joking about it. He did indeed soon become the starter for the Giants and played in 133 games. He hit fewer home runs than some years with only six, but brought in forty-five RBIs. Even though that was unquestionably overshadowed by Barry Bonds' 137 RBIs and record-setting seventy-three home runs, Benito was still the fifth highest on the team. And, as he had learned long before, his hitting ability wasn't as important as his catching skill and managing the pitchers. In the defensive role that had made his reputation, he still wowed the crowds when he hurled the ball to a base ahead of a runner with seeming ease. "The fans, they loved to see me throw from my knees. Sure, I liked to hear them cheer and I knew what they wanted, but it was never for show. My decision about how to throw hadn't changed from making that split-second choice about what had the best chance of getting a runner out. That's was what I was there for, not to entertain the crowd. When I could do both at the same time—sure, it was great. Risking an out to get their reaction—no, I wouldn't do that. It was funny, though, about the knees that was like my logo. When I traveled to Japan, there were some guys on the street wearing really nice, expensive suits and they stopped right there on the sidewalk and got down on their knees to imitate throwing before they shook my hand and asked to take a photo with me. Man, that was kind of crazy. I'm thinking about how they're going to ruin their suits, but they didn't seem to care."

There were plenty of hometown and nearby fans who came to the games, and as with other major cities close to the entertainment world, television cameras would especially focus in on different celebrities as commentators often pointed them out. "During my time in San Francisco, I had an opportunity to meet a lot of famous people. Robin Williams invited me to spend time with him. I met his son, and he would encourage me to play my best. It affected me when he [Williams] died because I spent some great time with him. I also had some time with Danny Glover. I had to take advantage of the times when I had a chance to talk with celebrities, and they always encouraged me to play my best. What was amazing to me is they always wanted to have their photo taken with me. In looking back on it, I wish I had taken some photos of me with them, but it wasn't easy when I was getting ready for games. That was where my focus needed to be."

His focus definitely paid off. More importantly than his statistics for his first season was an award that might be internal to the Giants, yet it was a clear signal to Benito that his feeling of San Francisco being the right team for him at that moment in time was correct. Each season, Giants players, coaches, training staff, and fans vote for one player to receive the "Willie Mac Award" named in honor of the very same Willie McCovey Benito met his first day in the clubhouse alongside Willie Mays. The award is given to the player viewed as the most inspirational to the team. The choice for 2001 was Benito. "I was honored because I got it as one of the all-around best players, and I didn't know in advance that I was going to receive the award. Because it was associated with Willie McCovey, that made it more special. I went back to the locker room to share the news with my teammates and to thank them. It was a good honor for me, and it inspired me. This ties in with the large Latino fan base and how this influenced me to play harder to perform for all the fans, but especially to bring pride to Latinos. I loved San Francisco."

Dusty Baker felt it was a deserved award. "Benito is one of the best people—always had a smile on his face—a guy you're glad to see. He had a special talent, too. I can't remember exactly who it was, but we had called a pitcher up from the minors and he was talking with Benito. When a pitcher and catcher first get together, the pitcher explains his habits—how he throws so the catcher knows what to expect and they don't get crossed up. Benito listened for a couple of minutes, then he said, 'Don't worry about that. I can catch anything you throw.' And the thing is he could. You don't see that in many catchers."

With his personal performance back in top form, a season finish of 90-72, and second place in the National League West, Benito and the team looked forward to the 2002 season. Winning the opening game always gives a boost. Five more back-to-back wins followed, and only seven games of the entire regular season were without runs. There were a few three- and four-game losing streaks, none of which took away from the growing belief that the Giants would make post-season. Benito was hitting well with more home runs and RBIs than in 2001, although not as strong as in that one remarkable season in Philadelphia. His performance was solid, and even though his appearance in the 2002 All-Star Game came through fan selection this time, it was as much a thrill as it had been his previous four selections. "After everything that had happened to me, I didn't know if I would be in another All-Stars, so I thought of it as very special. Too bad some of the four doctors who had thought I would never play again couldn't have been there."

Near mid-August, the Giants were four games back in the National League wild-card chase, then a string of wins pulled them ahead. It had been thirteen years since the team had played in a World Series, and a certain amount of tension was to be expected mixed with determination to keep the momentum going. Tempers had been sparked in the September 15th game against the San Diego Padres with what the Giants had protested as two particularly questionable calls. In the ninth inning, a heated dispute with the umpire got Dusty Baker, the manager; Dave Righetti, the pitching coach; and Benito all ejected. Photographs from that encounter captured the intense emotions. Benito held back from making public comments, but other teammates were vocal about their frustration. Benito's words to the umpire had only been heard between the two of them, and if as alleged, probably couldn't have been printed by reporters anyway—at least not without special characters being inserted as substitutes for certain words.

Despite that loss, the Giants grabbed a wild-card spot and didn't let the fact that they were underdogs to the favored Atlanta Braves deter them. They shocked Atlanta's hometown fans as well as predictions when they won Game One. The Braves recovered from their surprise and hammered out the next two wins to make it a go-big-or-go-home situation for the Giants. They came through, and with the outcome riding on Game Five, the narrow 3-1 victory over the Braves counted just as much as if it had been a blow-out. Benito and the team now faced the St. Louis Cardinals for the pennant and the coveted chance at the World Series. As they had done in Atlanta, the Giants took Game One and topped that by winning Game Two as well. The Cardinals weren't about to go down without a fight, and they pulled out a one-run win on the Giants' home field.

It was Game Four and even though Benito had played hundreds of times as a professional, he stepped to the plate for what became one of the greatest memories of his career. There was no question Barry Bonds was considered the biggest threat as a hitter by every team he played against, and he'd been walked multiple times in the series. In the eighth inning, the call was to walk Bonds, putting Benito at bat. This was nothing unexpected for Benito, and after having struck out earlier, he was concentrating on everything he knew about the pitcher. He was fully aware of the Cardinals' expectation that they had made the right decision to not let Bonds come in swinging at this critical point in the game. "You don't always know for sure, but there are other times when you feel it as soon as you connect and you know the ball is gone." As fast as the ball was moving, the crowd leaping to their feet screaming with joy was almost as fast. For Benito, it was one run that brought his team closer to the cherished dream of the World Series and gained him recognition as the Most Valuable Player of the series.

Game Five was it. Both teams were on the brink. The innings dragged with little scoring, and in classic baseball drama, victory finally went to the Giants. Not with a grand slam or anything close to it, but that didn't matter. "Man, the fifth game was tough with no home runs and not much in the way of hits, but all you need is one run more at the end. We got that, and everybody was going crazy. We were running onto the field, and everyone was pounding everyone on the back. My head was swimming, and I think it had to be the same for all the guys. You're so excited to realize you did it—you won the pennant and you're going to the World Series. For a player, it's a feeling that's hard to describe. I was a kid all those years ago, dreaming of being in a World Series, and now it was happening. Yes, it took me fifteen years, but some players in the Hall of Fame have never been."

Dusty Baker recalls that memorable time, "I don't think we would have made it to the Series without Benito."

Like the Giants, the Anaheim Angels came to the 2002 World Series through the wild-card route. Even though each team and their fans always root for a quick sweep, it's difficult to deny the value of a full seven-game battle. Setting aside the tremendous monetary advantage, anticipation heightens as the wins go back and forth and no one ever knows which way it will go despite hours spent in speculation. Of the seventeen four-game sweeps since 1907, the last had been in 1999 when the Yankees took the Series from the Braves. "If I could have had a choice, I really wanted us to play against the Yankees because of all the history, but it was the Angels," Benito recalled with a smile. "The West Coast version of a 'Subway Series,' I guess you could say."

Just as with the All-Star Games, there were activity-filled days leading up to the actual Series. "It's this huge celebration for everyone who loves baseball, and there are people who don't watch games the rest of the year who want to be part of it for that time. There are two days for enjoyment, and you have the first game the third day. We had all these events with lots of appearances and big parties to meet so many different people. You look around, see who's who, and there are plenty of things for the fans to do. That's also when you get many retired, famous players who come and you have a chance to talk to them and hear their stories. We were close to Disneyland so we went there, too, and spent some time."

In the technical sense, the Series is like any other game—the same number of players, the same distance between the bases, the two teams swap between their familiar home fields. As with every sport, though, when you are playing for the world championship, there is nothing "same" about it. "The atmosphere was tremendous, just to be inside the stadium—everything was a different feel. When you see that many people in the stands, it's unbelievable—what an experience to be there with the best players in the world. I was feeling like a kid; such enthusiasm, the expectations—and that's before you play the game. You get nervous, even after all the years of playing."

The 2002 World Series went to seven games. The Angels didn't find advantage on their home field with a win for each team. They had a convincing win by six runs in Game Three, but San Francisco got that single extra hit they needed for Game Four. The resounding Giants 16-4 victory in Game Five was everything they could have asked for. Benito easily remembered the confidence flowing through the locker room before Game Six began. This was the one that would clinch the Series for them. "We had the champagne iced down. We were sure this was it and we'd be champions. We had a chance, and you already think about how you're going to react. I decided I was going to knock down the pitcher. I could see myself running to do that, but we lost—6-5. We scored the first run, and then it didn't come together. We were six outs away from being World Champions, and those innings were some of the longest of my career. It goes back to the seventh to ninth innings being as important as they are. By losing Game Six, we would have to play Game Seven away and most of the time the home team wins. That's how it was for us. You'll never have another experience like it. There's no way for me not to feel like we should have won—that will stay with me forever, but so will the experience."

Disappointment washed over the city, but, hey—there was always next season. Except making it to the Series wasn't enough to overcome other issues, and Dusty Baker, the man who had brought Benito to San Francisco, was out for 2003. With the new manager, the team did win one hundred games to finish first in the National League West only to fall to the Marlins in the division series. New managers often bring a shuffling of players, and although Benito's eleven home runs and fifty-six RBIs in 2003 gave him a .279, in October he became a free agent again and his time in California was at an end.

Benito as a child in Puerto Rico with Nelida Gonzalez
(Photo from Benito Santiago's personal collection)

Benito positioned behind home plate with the San Diego Padres.
(Photographer: Stephen Dunn; Licensed through Getty Images Sports)

Benito Meets President Ronald Reagan during the 1989 season opener for the
San Diego Padres.
(Photo from Benito Santiago's personal collection)

President H.W Bush signs bat for Benito in his first All-Star Game (1989).
(Photo from Benito Santiago's personal collection)

Benito's 1996 year of 30 home runs with the Philadelphia Phillies
(Photographer: The Sporting News; Licensed through Getty Images Sports)

The Giants win the 2002 National League Pennant and go to the World Series.
(Photographer: Robert Beck; Licensed through Getty Images Sports)

Chapter Eleven
The Hardest Good-bye

The simple fact is the phrase, "Wait until next year/season," is an absolute among fans no matter the sport, city, or country. The words are spoken in many different languages for two purposes. If it's been a great season, there's hope for a repeat. If it's been a disappointing one, there's certainty the new season will be better. Kansas City Royals fans had experienced that roller-coaster effect of a strong 2003 season following a 62-100 record in 2002. Bringing in Tony Peña as the new manager was one of several off-season changes as was moving spring training from Florida to Arizona for the first time in the history of the team. There was still a lot of young blood on the team combined with some proven players, and the elements came together for spirit-lifting results. Their 83-79 record gave them a third-place finish in the division, Peña was named American League Manager of the Year, and their shortstop took the honor of Rookie of the Year. Fans were understandably looking forward to what 2004 would bring, and among the young players was now the veteran Benito Santiago. The nail-biting Opening Day game against the Chicago White Sox turned with a couple of thrilling home runs, and Benito was hitting well with three RBIs. The optimism generated in the early weeks started to slide as losses piled up. Preseason predictions of taking the American League Central Division disappeared along with Peña as manager. Benito had little playing time as it turned out, and the team finished with only fifty-eight wins.

Benito Santiago with Charlie Hudson

"Yeah, I had a couple of injuries, but it was more than that and I didn't want to think about what might be happening to me. I wasn't recovering the way I should have, and it was becoming harder for me to keep in shape. Kansas City was a beautiful place, but my time there didn't have anything special that stood out regarding the game. I loved the food there. I wish we had won the World Series like they did later, but the high hopes we had coming into the season didn't hold up. And it was funny in a way. I missed the Giants and coach more than I expected to, more than I had when changing from other teams. It was really the first time I had that kind of feeling. Going to a new team before had always pretty much been just another business decision."

In an unexpected development, the Pittsburgh Pirates reached out to make a deal for the veteran catcher, and Benito found himself in Pennsylvania once more for what was to be a mere six games. He became ill at the beginning of the season, and it didn't take long to realize the situation wasn't going to work for either party. Despite a quick departure and signing with the New York Mets in June, that was an even shorter venture.

"Here, I made it to a New York team to play baseball, and it was the wrong time of my career. I guess that's irony for you. I went to minor league in Norfolk with the Mets and my shoulder was finally bothering me, but I wouldn't tell anyone—I would throw and hop the ball—not me, I didn't do that. After two weeks, they said they were going to keep me in the minors, and I said, 'No, let me go home instead.' After I left, I'm thinking, 'What have I done?' Maybe I should have gone to the trainer and admitted the problem to see if he could help, but I refused to complain. I was sure they would cut me if I did. It was difficult for me to accept my shoulder was hurting because I'd been warned about it for years and never had to worry about it. I got plenty of rest and my velocity came back, but I was starting to feel the effects of living in a suitcase and flying all the time. I was getting tired. I could tell that it was time for me to hand the glove and bat over and go home. I felt bad for the fans, but I couldn't avoid the reality."

At age forty, Benito's remarkable playing run was over. From the teenager who was brought up through the minors, to the man who had played in the World Series, the summer of 2005 did not include Benito Santiago as a professional baseball player.

"You know it's going to end someday. I watched so many players leave who got hurt, or couldn't stick with it in the majors, or who finally had to retire. I played longer than a lot of them, but then it was my turn to hang up the uniform. My whole life from when I was a kid had been baseball. It didn't mean I had to leave the game for good, but it did mean whatever came next wouldn't be as a player."

Before his resurgence with the Giants, when he wasn't certain if he would fully recover from the accident, Benito had purchased land in Puerto Rico. It included acreage on a peak with a panoramic view above Santa Isabel, his childhood home. It was undeveloped, yet he knew it could be a special place for him someday.

"I had different things I could do, but working with kids has always been something I enjoyed and it was something to think about. I went to Florida and was in the Fort Lauderdale and Pompano Beach areas. I took some time off and later went to the Dominican Republic to a baseball academy for a while. I made several trips back and forth to Puerto Rico. It's funny, but I didn't have anything specific in mind I wanted to do."

Chapter Twelve
When Scandal Looms

As a professional athlete, there is no shortage of events—personal and professional—that can blossom into scandal. In either case, you can depend on headlines. What you don't always get are ramifications that shake an entire sport. The steroids scandal in baseball that sparked and then exploded with ferocity came in the waning years of Benito's career.

"Look, you hear all this talk and the worry about steroids and, okay, the League sets up rules. If there really was some magic drug, don't you think there would be more superstars in sports? Wouldn't everyone just use that and be great? After my accident, I was in a lot of pain for a long time. I was taking multiple medications, and I did different things to recover, to prove I could still play the game. The old Benito wasn't gone, and I wasn't going to quit. Most players use more than one kind of supplements and don't ask a lot of questions about what they are. Anyone who thinks the only reason I played as well as I did in San Francisco was because of steroids doesn't understand anything about me."

When whispers turn to open talk, it's difficult to know what the depth and duration of the scandal will be. How many people will be caught up in it, who they will be, who will fall, who will survive? At a minimum, a major scandal ripples through the media, the fans, and the structure of the teams. In other cases, a scandal becomes a flood instead of a ripple, and the destructive potential can be alarming. In the

2000s, multiple events about illegal steroid use swept in names from virtually every level of professional baseball as the U.S. Congress and others initiated investigations. Allegations and actions took place over an extended period of five years and ignited heated discussions throughout the country. Thousands of pages of official reports, articles, and several books were written, and there was no shortage of opinions about what was true and what was seen as "witch-hunting." In looking back at some of the major pieces of the drama, the use of performance enhancing drugs (PEDs) was not a new concern. If you search through history, you can find references as early as the original Olympics more than 2,700 years ago. Coming a bit more into the present, the International Association of Amateur Federations (IAAF) was established in 1912 following the close of the summer Olympics. Although it was intended to govern track and field, it changed over the decades and the name became Association of Athletics Federations. The issue of using drugs to enhance sports performance was addressed in 1928 when the federation formally adopted a rule against "doping" and it continues to stress the need for strict testing and control.

Stories about the use of drugs in Major League Baseball date back to at least the 1950s. One of the first official mentions of steroids as PEDs was apparently raised in a letter from West Virginia Congressman Harley Staggers to the Commissioner of Baseball. That particular exchange did not lead to significant changes, but anabolic steroids were added to the Schedule III of the Controlled Substances Act in the Anabolic Steroid Control Act of 1990. The following year, Baseball Commissioner Fay Vincent established a policy that said, "The possession, sale, or use of any illegal drug or controlled substance by Major League players and personnel is strictly prohibited. This prohibition applies to all illegal drugs and controlled substances, including steroids."

Although this was the type of statement those who had concerns wanted to see, many were convinced the procedures for drug testing and the actions to be taken if a player violated the policy would not be effective. Various health impacts such as heart problems and liver damage are cited by medical experts as dangers, and use among youth caused special alarm. The position that players who use steroids (to include human growth hormone) provide unfair advantage over players who "stay clean" was another important factor to steroid opponents.

Periodic articles addressed the persistent rumors, and in 2001 MLB established testing procedures in the minor league. The owners came to agreement with the Major League Baseball Players Association [the players' union] in 2002 to begin selected testing in 2003, although there was again criticism that the procedures were not likely to be effective.

By mid-2003, a scandal centered in San Francisco was breaking loose as the news media became aware of a major investigation into the Bay Area Laboratory Co-operative (BALCO). The company was connected to not only the San Francisco Giants, but also to other teams, sports, and Olympic athletes. There were allegations of the creation of designer steroids that could not be detected by normal testing. After federal and local agencies raided BALCO in September 2003, a federal grand jury was convened in December, and Benito was among the San Francisco Giants players called in to testify.

"I wasn't there to talk about anyone except me. They want to know about the other players, that wasn't for me to say. Sometimes, they ask the same question different ways, but I wasn't going to make comments outside of what I did."

Not surprisingly, the scandal erupted when the grand jury testimony was illegally leaked to a journalist and the list of famous athletes involved grew. Then in early 2005, Jose Canseco's book,

Juiced: Wild Times, Rampant 'Roids, Smash Hits, and How Baseball Got Big, made even bigger headlines. As had happened in the past, the U.S. Congress exercised its authority and officially stepped into the controversy. A March 2005 memorandum issued to members of the Committee on Government Reform contained this opening paragraph:

"Major League Baseball is a multibillion-dollar industry that enjoys extensive public subsidies, tax breaks, and an exemption from antitrust laws. Over the past decade, credible allegations of widespread use of anabolic steroids by ballplayers have cast a cloud over the sport. The Committee's investigation aims to shed light on what happened and how it happened in order to assess the adequacy of federal laws on controlled substances, educate the public about the dangers to youth who may be tempted to use anabolic steroids, and ensure that adequate safeguards for the future are in place."

Another page of the memorandum cited concern with MLB's attention to the issue. Baseball finally reached an agreement with the players' union to initiate anonymous testing during the 2003 season. Under this policy, the testing did not occur during the off-season, when most steroid use is believed to occur, and did not include all anabolic steroids. According to information provided by Major League Baseball, 5–7 percent of players tested positive in 2003. In 2004, a similar testing program was administered confidentially, with the positive rates falling to 1–2 percent.

In January 2005, Baseball Commissioner Bud Selig announced a new testing policy that he claimed would "eradicate" steroid use. The effectiveness of this new initiative was a significant focus of the hearing. Benito was not brought in as a witness, although some of his former teammates from other teams were. Even though the final Congressional report did not specify changes that should be made to the MLB drug testing policies, Commissioner Selig took an unusual, additional step with regard to the allegations. He contacted former

U.S. Senator George J. Mitchell and requested that he conduct a separate comprehensive investigation into the use of steroids and human growth hormone.

Once again, there was no shortage of opinions as to whether this action should have been taken, but it was. The massive report was 409 pages when completed, took more than twenty months to complete, and was publicly released in December 2007. Benito was not among those interviewed, but his testimony in BALCO was cited in one of the many recorded documents. The entire report can be found online, and the scope was greater than many had anticipated. Mitchell engaged a law firm and a variety of medical and sports experts. He and his team reviewed more than 115,000 pages of documents from the commissioner's office and the thirty clubs as well as over twenty thousand electronic documents. Other sources were also used and more than seven hundred witnesses in the United States, Canada, and the Dominican Republic were interviewed. The majority interviewed were past and present club officials, managers, coaches, team physicians, athletic trainers, or resident security agents. Members of the commissioner's office were among the interviewees, and of nearly five hundred players they approached, only sixty-eight agreed to talk to them.

Not surprisingly, there was criticism and praise for the report, and changes were made to testing policies and punishment for violation of those policies. A number of careers were impacted in different ways, one of which was to essentially eliminate the chances of being voted into the National Baseball Hall of Fame for certain players who would otherwise be considered.

It was, and continues to be, a consequence Benito disapproves of. "Think about this. The best baseball players of my era are fighting to get into the Hall of Fame and can't because of the steroid situation. My knees were bad and they recommended steroids, plus this all came up at the end of my career. Let's not talk about if I ever had a real chance at the Hall of Fame, but so many really good players are excluded—not officially, but everyone knows that's why. Roger Clemens and Barry Bonds for example. Whether or not they even used steroids is just one question. You think what they were able to do was all because of steroids? How would that even be possible? It doesn't make sense to think like that. Out of all the players during my time who deserved the Hall of Fame and were caught up in the scandal, Mike Piazza is the first one who's finally in. I hope the other guys eventually make it. The new testing they've gone to might solve the problem—it's hard to say. Maybe after a while, people will look back and see they overreacted."

As far as the impact on the fans, they were faced with making personal determinations as to how they viewed players who were named in the report. Was all the great hitting during what became known as the "Steroids Era" due to the use of performance enhancing drugs? If not all, then how much? A little, some? No matter how many thousands of conversations took place arguing both sides of the issue, attendance at Major League games did not decrease after the scandals broke.

Major League Baseball did initiate a number of changes after the report was completed, but based on periodic headlines since that time, the use of performance enhancing drugs in whatever form they take is a subject that might continue to surface as long as professional sports are multibillion-dollar businesses where competitive edges are constantly sought.

Chapter Thirteen
Honors Bestowed

Being selected into the National Baseball Hall of Fame is a fantasy of children who aspire to baseball as a profession and a dream shared by the most seasoned players. Even though the physical museum did not open until 1939, in 1936 the five great names of Ty Cobb, Walter Johnson, Christy Mathewson, Babe Ruth, and Honus Wagner were inducted. As of 2016, there have been 312 individuals honored: 217 as players, 28 executives who made significant contributions, 35 from the Negro Leagues, 22 managers, and even 10 umpires. There are only five MLB teams to date that have not had a member entered into the National Hall of Fame, and while most avid baseball fans make or at least plan a visit to Cooperstown, New York, someday, there are also nine specific major league team Halls of Fame. Then there are state, city, or regional Sports Halls of Fame where men and women across the sports spectrum are recognized. In some cases, there are other country or special associations that establish a Hall of Fame such as the Hispanic Heritage Baseball Museum and Hall of Fame established in San Francisco in 1999.

According to its website, "The Hispanic Heritage Baseball Museum is committed to preserving the history and profound influence that Hispanic players have had on 'America's Favorite Past Time.' Our primary purpose is to provide a center where displays of Hispanic baseball history will educate visitors on the true meaning of diversity, as exemplified in sports. We also offer traveling exhibitions of our prized collection throughout the year."

A short turn into the history of Hispanic or Latin players emphasizes the growth of their influence that Benito became a part of. There are several excellent books and multiple articles to read about the fascinating roots that began perhaps as early as the 1850s in Cuba. In 1864, Nemesio and Ernesto Guilló established the Havana Baseball Club, and with two other clubs in place in 1878, the Cuban League drew large crowds. The game's popularity spread through the Caribbean into Mexico, Nicaragua, Venezuela, Puerto Rico, the Dominican Republic, and other countries. There were increases of Latino players in the United States, and in one of the quirks of history, since Cubans weren't subject to the draft for the U.S. military and other Latino countries weren't in general heavily involved in World War II, a number of MLB teams augmented their rosters with Latino players.

There was, however, the cultural issue of segregation which was not something present in the players' home countries. Up to 15 percent of players in the Negro Leagues were Latino, and those who were lighter-skinned were the ones brought onto major league teams. When Jackie Robinson broke the color barrier in 1947 with the Brooklyn Dodgers, it opened the way for across-the-board change. Of note, however, is in the world of baseball that is business, Latino players were often signed at a lower salary for a variety of reasons. This was common, if unpublicized, knowledge and continued for as long as team owners could manage to do so. The great Roberto Clemente, Orlando Cepeda, and Louis Arapicio, all later elected to the National Hall of Fame, helped signal the permanence of Latino players in the league. Benito and his peers were still on the leading edge of what has become close to 30 percent of MLB players. The particular timing of being in a distinct minority during much of his career caused Benito's periodic sense of isolation. The other side of that coin, though, was it also meant he was a role model for so many young players who saw him unquestionably achieve their own dream.

The founder, president, and CEO of HHBM, Gabriel (Tito) Avila Jr., had followed Benito's career from early on. "I met Benito through my brother, Raymond. My brother and I went to so many of his games and had good times together. Benito has been a great example for kids to see, and watching him play was always a pleasure. I was in the stands when he hit the first home run in the history of the Marlins team. The way that ball flew was terrific, and the fans were cheering. It was an experience you always remember."

There was to be a ten-year reunion of the 2002 World Series Giants team in 2012, and what could be a better time to induct Benito into the Hispanic Heritage Baseball Museum and Hall of Fame? The ceremony took place July 1, 2012, prior to the Giants-Cincinnati game, which the Giants won. Even though Benito had played twice for Cincinnati, the Giants and San Francisco were an indelible part of his past.

"I had no idea how I was voted in. Tito contacted me to give me the news. The ceremony was very special to me because there are a lot of Latinos in San Francisco, so getting this honor there made it more significant to me. I have a lot of respect for that area, and so I played hard when I was there. They have some of the best fans. I loved it there. Later, the Hispanic Hall of Fame had a spot at the San Diego Convention Center during the 2016 All-Star Game, and I enjoyed seeing that, too."

Three years after that honor, Benito was in California again. This occasion was also in San Diego for another emotional ceremony. The team that had brought Benito across the Caribbean and the country for a chance at a childhood dream was preparing to induct him into their Hall of Fame. The city, which had been granted an expansion team in 1968, saw the inaugural game April 8, 1969, with a slim win over

Houston. More than twenty-three thousand fans cheered, a fraction of the number who would attend in the coming decades. The question in 1974 of whether the team would be moved to Washington, DC was settled when Ray Kroc, the man who founded McDonalds, purchased the team to ensure it remained in San Diego. He did not live to see them take the National League Pennant in 1984 and go to the World Series, but his widow maintained his legacy until the Tom Werner Group purchased the team in 1990. It was 1999 in commemoration of their thirtieth anniversary when the first members of the San Diego Padres Hall of Fame were inducted; they included Randy Jones (pitcher), Nate Colbert (first base), and Ray Kroc (former owner). Only nine other players had been inducted, when in 2015, Benito and Garry Templeton were inducted. For Benito, being there with Templeton added to the honor.

"When we played for the Padres, Garry taught me a lot about the game and he also taught me a lot about family. He had me spend time with his family, and he was one of the guys who really found a balance between being dedicated to the game and his family. Templeton was shortstop, and Alomar played second base. Alomar was exciting at second base, and it was a good combination we had. We were both glad to see Alomar go into the National Hall of Fame. For me, though, it was special to be inducted into the Padres Hall of Fame with Templeton at the same time since we had such a strong bond when we played together."

There was another irony since Templeton was a shortstop—the position Benito might well have played had he not unexpectedly put on that catcher's gear that day in Puerto Rico. As with most of these ceremonies, it was conducted as a pregame event, this one on the day the Padres were up against the Philadelphia Phillies, one of Benito's other former teams.

"You come to the games like this where a lot of veterans show up and you see people you haven't seen in years. It's a great time for remembering, and I have to admit it was kind of good to hear that my thirty-four-game hitting streak still holds the record as the longest in Padres' history. I know someone will break it one of these days, but it's been almost thirty years, so that's not bad."

Among the activities, Benito was invited into the broadcast booth with Jesse Agler and Mark Grant. "Oh, man, it was great being up there with those guys. I had to admit I was a little nervous about the whole ceremony; I hadn't been in front of a camera for a while. They had a video clip of me throwing from my knees to get a runner out. Wow, we were all so young then, and I had to wonder where the years went. It didn't seem possible so much time had gone by. Mark was talking about when he came to the Padres as a pitcher, and I told him not to worry about getting runners out. That was my job. What he had to do was concentrate on his pitching and strikes. He was good to catch for, and I had fun talking in the booth. I told them about the baseball academy in the Dominican Republic I was working with and how it would be nice for me to have a kid make it to the majors someday."

Fans were given a choice of jerseys for the game and the name *Santiago* was frequently seen as cameras swept around for crowd shots. The acknowledgment and events stirred emotions and brought memories into focus. What amazing years those had been and what a life it had been the beginning of. From the nervous teenager taking his first airplane trip through the tough conditions in the minors, there had definitely been downturns along the way, but here he was standing on the field as his list of accomplishments drew applause.

Perhaps it was time to capture the story of those memories and the tumultuous life that could have ended in tragic death instead of being embraced by the Gonzalez family. Benito knew he was by no means the only player to have come from poverty and complicated family situations. He had, however, stepped back and taken accounting of all that had happened to him. His was a story with enough common elements among those that were unique to help provide a guide for the kids who shared his dream and, more importantly, for those who might step into the spotlight of professional baseball, unprepared for the demanding realities of fame. "It isn't easy to think about admitting your mistakes, but now that I'm older, I can see if I had known, maybe I would have made some other decisions. Maybe it won't make a difference to some because we don't always want to listen. If I write this book, though, and talk about how it was for me, and it helps only a few kids, that's still good. And there were a lot of wonderful things, funny things people can laugh about. People who loved me, supported me, and gave me chances—I can let them know how much it meant to me."

Not that it would be a tell-all with the kind of stories that tabloids either seek out or make up. "Hey, some of the crazy things, I don't want to get into those. The people who were with me know what happened, and they want to talk about it, they can write their own book."

In many ways, the mask Benito wore as a catcher symbolized events in his life. The secrets of his early childhood masked, not as deception, but to protect him until he was old enough to grasp the truth. His too frequent angry outbursts during his career masked the intense cultural and language obstacles that prevented him from being able to express himself in the appropriate way. The pain he masked as he fought back from the terrible accident that could have left him a cripple. In coming to recognize the personal failings that accompanied the deeds he has every right to be proud of, the man behind the mask can tell his story that will no doubt be viewed in different ways according to each reader.

Chapter Fourteen
Reflections and the Next Stage

"My time with the major leagues had so many opportunities. I got to go to a lot of cities and meet a lot of people and experience their food and had people who came to see me and cheer me on. I also got to meet a lot of famous people, just because of the game that I played. It was one of the biggest experiences for me to go to New York, Chicago, and learn so much after coming from a small island. I spent a lot of good times with people, and I never dreamed of that when I was young. I mean, I dreamed of being in the major leagues, but you don't understand what all goes with that when you're a kid. The fans cheering, being rich, the cars you can buy, having your picture on a baseball card and people wanting your autograph, that's what you're thinking about. The idea of having players like Johnny Bench sitting down with you to give you pointers, or handing your jacket to a famous actor like Andy García, or having Muhammad Ali talk to you about your career, isn't what comes into your mind. I have a bat signed by President Bush, the senior one, and I talked about spending time with Robin Williams. It is something that I will take with me until I die."

Having played on the West Coast, in the Midwest, and in Canada, Benito chose to live in South Florida in the Fort Lauderdale and Pompano Beach areas after he retired. Somehow, seventeen years slipped past as he worked with baseball academies in Puerto Rico and the Dominican Republic. The age group he prefers is fourteen to sixteen where he feels he can do the most good. "I think it's great for kids of any age to play baseball, to have fun with it. You can make great memories from Little League. The body and muscles have to develop, though, and you can't really tell what a kid will be like until a little later and it's easy for younger kids to lose interest and go on to something different. The older kids are where I can help the most. I can see if there is real talent and the potential to move up. I would love that—to have a kid go to the majors and know I was a part of it."

Benito also knows the odds are against most of them; that hasn't changed over the decades. When do you break the news? "You have to be willing to be honest about this and tell the truth. If you don't, it will come back on you. There are people who will keep encouraging a kid even when they know he doesn't have a real chance, and I learned you can't do that. It isn't fair to anyone. You have to be careful, though, because there isn't one single right way of teaching. Sometimes you have a kid who doesn't respond to one way and you can make some adjustment and bring him along if the talent is there. I'm not saying I am always right, but I put my ability to judge a kid's potential up against almost anyone I know. It's easy to tell a kid and his parents if you think he has a real shot. That makes everyone feel good. If you've tried different ways and it isn't working, it's hard to have that conversation, but you have to be honest if you don't see it in a kid. Maybe you want to tell him privately first or with his parents, but you can't keep pretending he'll get better. You don't want to turn them against baseball. Just because I don't think he can go all the way doesn't mean he can't play well enough to get a scholarship to college or maybe even get into the minors if that's what he wants to do. You have to make sure they understand the options. If he or the parents don't want to believe me and go to another coach, that's okay, I understand."

An aspect he does worry about with the hopefuls in Puerto Rico is the impact of the 1990 decision to include Puerto Rico in MLB's first-year player draft. This means Puerto Rican players must wait until they have completed high school to sign a professional contract, and then they are in competition with every other high school player throughout the United States and sometimes those who are in junior colleges. "There are people who say it doesn't make a difference, and I completely disagree with that. Like when I was a kid, we had these scouts because they knew they could come watch us young and sign us up early. With being part of the bigger draft, why spend time on the island targeting a player when every other team is going to be looking at him too for the draft? I have to advise parents if they can manage it to send their kid to school in the United States to give them a better chance to be noticed."

It's hard to know what other opportunities in addition to teaching may come, and Benito keeps himself in shape. "You don't want to let yourself go. I'm fifty-two and you put me on the field and I can still play nine innings. Not as quick as I was, but that's okay."

The professional side of this stage of his life is one thing. It is the personal side where Benito looks with regrets. "I've got four great kids, and it was because of their mothers, not me. I wasn't the kind of dad I should have been or could have been. I don't mean money—I always took care of that and made sure they had what they needed. A home, clothes, schools—you don't let your family do without those things. It was my time they didn't have. I wasn't there for them and wasn't a part of them growing up the way I could have been. Baseball was so important to me—winning and being Benito the catcher—and you think it's okay with the family. Or that's what you tell yourself. Maybe the divorce would have happened no matter what. We were really young when we got married. What I do know is like I said before, you get to be this big guy, this star, and you can get too wrapped up in that. I knew players who really did find the balance, and there were times when I did pay more attention to being with my family. It wasn't enough, though, and here I am trying to make up for that. I'm working hard to get to know my kids, to tell them about the mistakes I made. I don't want to be seventy and keep saying what I should have done to heal the breach."

His daughter Bennybeth, the child he had once thought for sure would be a boy, was the one who spent the most time with him as she lived for a number of years in Florida. She finally convinced her mother to make the move from California, yet being geographically closer to Benito didn't result in as close a relationship as it could have been. Her mother returned to Puerto Rico when her father became ill and stayed on the island. Bennybeth later joined her mother in Puerto Rico and lived there for a while with her and plenty of extended family around.

Despite some traveling, Benito is spending more time in Puerto Rico as well. In working on his memoirs, there have been photographs discovered, stories emerging, and questions asked that can be more easily answered than in the past. Not that the answers are easy, but Benito is committed to making the effort to explain.

Ties with his oldest son were strengthened when they had the chance to explore their shared passion for sports. Taller and more broad-shouldered at six five and over two hundred pounds, Benito Junior actually played both basketball and baseball for a bit at Lon Morris College in Jacksonville, Texas. With a young wife and baby to look after, he chose to leave school to go to Puerto Rico to work together with his dad in a baseball academy. Then the younger Santiago's love for basketball won out. He attended the University of the Cumberlands in Kentucky for a period of time as a key player on the school's team. He also played for the *Atleticos de San German* in the *Baloncesto Superior Nacional*, Puerto Rico's national basketball team. Founded in 1929, BSN has a regular season of thirty-six to forty-four games depending on the year, then the playoffs. They are known internationally, have participated in numerous Olympics, and sent several stars to the NBA. "When I'm in the stands, I think my son plays better, but that's how it's supposed to be. Right now, though, he's going through some personal stuff, and I can help him with that, too."

For those who long to see another generation of Santiago in a baseball uniform, that would be his youngest son, Benito Ivan, who is gaining lots of attention at the University of Tennessee. He's a catcher, even though he hasn't demonstrated the throw-from-his-knees form of his dad. Although it's too soon to know what his future holds, there is no question certain MLB teams are aware of him. "It's hard because I was never there for him when he was young. I mean here he is playing as a catcher and I wasn't the one coaching and teaching him. How crazy is that? He doesn't know what all happened between his mom and me, and he doesn't need to unless he wants to. I've reached out, and it will be slow, but we're starting to have maybe a chance to talk about things that are important. I have to be the one to tell him how proud I am of him and be willing to answer whatever it is he wants to know."

Aliyah Santiago Evans, his youngest daughter in Arizona, is still in high school and will probably go to college. "They are all smart and good kids, and I can't go back and change what happened. The best I can do is try and I know my explanations won't always sound good, but it's important I do this.

"The other good thing with my family is my mom, Nelida, the woman who took me in and was with me all my life. After Modesto died, I bought her a house in Coamo where she was originally from. It isn't the kind of great house I used to have, but she grew up really hard, very poor, so she doesn't want anything too big. She's a little slower now, but she's doing well and I see my sisters, too. I love my mom, and I'll do whatever I can for her. That family made me what I am."

Not a big house or like the one he used to have? What happened to the money? "This is one of the other things I want kids and parents to understand. I didn't make the kind of money you see now, but it was millions of dollars and I made so many mistakes I can't remember them all. You grow up poor and you don't know how to handle money, and neither does anyone you know. That's the truth of it. Suddenly, you have this contract, especially if the next one is bigger, and you think your problems are over, it will last forever. It doesn't, and sure, you start out and there's nothing wrong with buying the car, the house, the clothes, and other luxuries; helping your family, eating in fancy restaurants, being a big spender. You ought to enjoy it. You can do all that, though, and still be smart. It was like me with the cars. I loved cars, but how many do you need at one time? Why have more than two when you're going to want to buy newer ones later anyway? My agent Scott Boras tried to tell me, and I wouldn't listen. A good agent, one of the best things he can do for you is put you together with someone who knows how money works and how to manage it for the long term. You have to understand all kinds of people will come to you with ideas and it might sound good, but that doesn't mean they know what they're talking about. You get involved with something they tell you was a sure thing and it falls apart on you, and you think those same people are going to do anything about getting your money back? That's not going to happen. And when you want to take care of family and friends, you have to see it can start out to be a good thing, but maybe it gets out of hand. It's hard to realize sometimes people start to see you differently. They stop caring about you as a person and what they see then is just the money. You want to learn something really hard about people? That's it."

The sobering reality Benito learned is he is not unique in the way he lost so much money. Studies have shown a pattern among professional athletes: 50–60 percent become essentially broke within three to five years of retirement. "The point is you are the one who has to recognize what can happen and make the decision early to be smart about it. No one can make that choice for you."

In the time after the accident when his ability to walk again was in question and the opportunity to resume his career was in doubt, Benito did buy those parcels of land in Puerto Rico. The undeveloped one with the panoramic view above Santa Isabel, the town of his childhood, has potential. "I have a couple of deals working, and we'll see what happens with those. Land is a good investment, but you have to wait for the timing to work in your favor. You can't do anything to speed it up. You're stuck until the timing is right, and it could take years. If these deals come out good for me, I've learned my lesson and will be more careful from now on."

His love of baseball will never diminish although it seems as if it is more a big business than ever before. "The money is crazy big now, and I think it's changed the game—that's what they care about more than winning for the team. You make ninety million dollars and get a big amount up-front, if you don't play well, you still come out with a lot of money with only one year. Why should a player care? Yeah, my kid might be part of this and make a lot, but I still don't agree with it. Plus, used to, you get hurt—you might play through—now, you get hurt, you've already made money, why not walk away? And the signing bonuses, how does that make sense? Okay, if you have a big budget and you want to keep a guy you know can perform, you pay him. You want to give millions of dollars for a player who hasn't picked up a bat for you yet or thrown a pitch? Players don't always fit in a team, and if he doesn't, you've wasted that money."

In looking back and forward, for Benito, the love of the game itself won't fade. "People love baseball for a reason, and it's the hardest game to play. I know football is harder physically and basketball is a faster pace, but you go ask someone like Deion Sanders who played football as well and Michael Jordan who was as good at basketball as anyone and see if they don't agree with me. In baseball, you can't win unless you score, and you can't score unless you hit that ball. When you play as kids, that's one thing. You're only going to have so many good pitchers, and you might not run across a really good one until high school, college, or the minors. You get to the majors and the only way a pitcher makes it there is by beating out a lot of other good pitchers. A ball comes at you one-hundred-plus miles an hour and that's not like anything you can really imagine until you try it. Think about it. If you're batting .300, which is good but not great, that means you're only getting a hit one-third of the time you try. What teacher in school is going to say that's a rate to appreciate? And in playing defense, you have to always be watching in baseball because you never know where the ball is going. Okay, you have a real power hitter who sends it high over the fence and there's no way to stop it, but other times, you can misjudge and miss a catch because you didn't stretch an extra couple of inches. The other part is, I think the strategy is more intense, like talking about deciding to walk a hitter or not, or when to bunt. The bases being loaded makes decisions different than if no one is on base or maybe one runner is on first. As a catcher you're more aware of some of this, but for guys who love the game, they understand the whole game and the part they play in it."

Benito doesn't know what the future will bring. "I have my son who might make it to the majors, and I have three grandchildren. When I would get a ticket for my dad Modesto, the one who raised me, I could always tell that he was in the stands because he would make sure that he screamed and I could hear him over everyone else. It's my turn to do that for my sons, and maybe one or more of my grandchildren will have the baseball genes. That happens and you better believe I'll be there for them, screaming loud enough for them to hear me."

The End

Selected Statistics for Benito Santiago Career

Author's Note, Charlie Hudson

Although the love of statistics may not exactly flow through the veins of every baseball fan, it is an appropriate phrase. There are multiple sources of statistics and I am grateful for finding Retrosheet.org as a valuable source. In accessing the information used in this appendix, I am including the following statement:

"The information used here was obtained free of charge from and is copyrighted by Retrosheet. Interested parties may contact Retrosheet at "www.retrosheet.org"."

I am also including the statement of, "All information is subject to corrections as additional data are received. We are grateful to anyone who discovers discrepancies and we appreciate learning of the details." http://www.retrosheet.org/

Not all statistics displayed on Retrosheet are included in this appendix and the selected data included here was accessed August 29, 2016. The two sections contain portions of Benito's batting and fielding records. There is a section for Benito's regular season fielding record, followed by sections for the Divisional Series, the League Championship Series, the World Series and All-Star games, if applicable. For each section, the information included is what was available.

Regular Season, Division Series, League Championship Series, World Series, All-Star Games

Full name: Benito (Rivera) Santiago

Born: March 9, 1965, Ponce, Puerto Rico

First Game: September 14, 1986; Final Game: April 11, 2005

Bat: Right Throw; Right Height: 6' 1"; Weight: 180

Named NL Rookie of the Year by Baseball Writers' Association of America (1987)

Named NL Rookie Player of the Year by The Sporting News (1987)

Named NL League Championship Series Most Valuable Player (2002)

*Named catcher on The Sporting News NL All-Star Team (1987, 1989 and 1991)

Won NL Gold Glove as catcher (1988 to 1990)

Named catcher on The Sporting News NL Silver Slugger Team (1987 to 1988 and 1990 to 1991)

Ejections: 1993 (2), 1994 (1), 1996 (1), 2001 (2), 2002 (3), 2003 (1), 2004 (1). Total: 11

* Author's Note, Charlie Hudson:

Selected to 1990 All-Star Game and unable to play due to injury prior to game; He was in the 2002 game which made him one of only 10 MLB players to go to an All-Star Game 10 or more years after his last appearance.

Batting Record

G   - Games Played

AB - At Bats

R   - Runs Scored

H   - Hits

2B - Doubles

3B - Triples

HR - Home Runs

RBI - Runs Batted In

Year	Team	G	AB	R	H	2B	3B	HR	RBI
1986	SD (N)	17	62	10	18	2	0	3	6
1987	SD (N)	146	546	64	164	33	2	18	79
1988	SD (N)	139	492	49	122	22	3	10	46
1989	SD (N)	129	462	50	109	16	3	16	62
1990	SD (N)	100	344	42	93	8	5	11	53
1991	SD (N)	152	580	60	155	22	3	17	87
1992	SD (N)	106	386	37	97	21	0	10	42
Year	Team	G	AB	R	H	2B	3B	HR	RBI
1993	FLA (N)	139	469	49	108	19	6	13	50
1994	FLA (N)	101	337	35	92	14	2	11	41
1995	CIN (N)	81	266	40	76	20	0	11	85
1996	PHI (N)	136	481	71	127	21	2	30	85
1997	TOR (A)	97	341	31	83	10	0	13	42
1998	TOR (A)	15	29	3	9	5	0	4	1
1999	CHI (N)	109	350	28	87	18	3	7	36
2000	CIN (N)	89	252	22	66	11	1	8	45
2001	SF (N)	133	477	39	125	25	4	6	45
2002	SF (N)	126	478	56	133	24	5	16	74
2003	SF (N)	108	401	53	112	21	2	11	56
2004	KC (A)	49	175	15	48	10	0	6	23
2005	PIT (N)	6	23	1	6	1	1	0	0
Total NL (17 years); Total AL (3 years); Total MLB (20 years)									

Division Series Batting Record

Year	Team	G	AB	R	H	2B	3B	HR	RBI
1995	CIN (N)	3	9	2	3	0	0	1	3
2002	SF (N)	5	21	1	5	2	0	0	5
2003	SF (N)	4	11	0	2	0	0	0	0

League Championship Series Batting Record

Year	Team	G	AB	R	H	2B	3B	HR	RBI
1995	CIN (N)	4	13	0	3	0	0	0	0
2002	SF (N)	5	20	2	6	0	0	2	6

World Series Batting Record

Year	Team	G	AB	R	H	2B	3B	HR	RBI
2002	SF (N)	7	26	2	6	0	0	0	5

*All-Star Game Batting Record

Year	Team	G	AB	R	H	2B	3B	HR	RBI
1989	NL	1	1	0	0	0	0	0	0
1991	NL	1	3	0	0	0	0	0	0
1992	NL	1	1	0	0	0	0	0	0
2002	NL	1	2	0	1	0	0	0	0
*Selected to 1990 All Star Game and unable to play due to injury prior to game									

Fielding Record

POS - Defensive Position

G   - Games Played

GS   - Games Started

CG   - Complete Games (for OF, this is the sum of his CGs at LF, CF and RF, and will not include CGs in the OF at more than one position)

PO - Putouts

A   - Assists

E   - Errors

DP - Double Plays

TP - Triple Plays

PB - Passed Balls

SB - Stolen Bases Allowed

CS - Caught Stealing

PkO - PickOffs

Year	Team	POS	G	GS	CG	PO	A	ERR	DP	TP	PB	SB	CS	PkO
1986	SD	C	17	15	14	80	7	5	2	0	3	14	3	1
1987	SD	C	146	140	130	817	80	22	12	0	22	104	50	6
1988	SD	C	136	128	125	725	75	12	11	0	9	57	46	9
1989	SD	C	151	148	138	685	81	20	10	0	14	46	32	15
1990	SD	C	98	89	84	538	51	12	6	0	6	60	31	4
1991	SD	C	151	148	138	830	100	14	14	0	8	93	57	1
1991	SD	LF	1	0	0	0	0	0	0	0				
1991	SD	OF	1	0	0	0	0	0	0	0	1	0	0	
1992	SD	C	103	98	91	584	53	12	6	0	0	73	42	0
1993	FLA	C	136	125	114	740	64	11	4	0	23	90	39	7
1993	FLA	LF	1	0	0	0	0	0	0	0				
1993	FLA	OF	1	0	0	0	0	0	0	0	1	0	0	
1994	FLA	C	97	88	86	511	66	5	6	0	6	45	40	2
1995	CIN	C	75	71	60	461	33	2	4	0	6	34	13	1
1995	CIN	1B	8	1	1	19	2	0	2	0				
1996	PHI	C	114	112	110	723	61	10	5	0	8	64	28	1
1996	PHI	1B	14	12	12	111	6	1	9	0				
1997	TOR	C	95	93	89	621	40	2	10	0	7	48	31	2
1997	TOR	DH	1	1	1									
1998	TOR	C	15	6	5	45	2	0	0	0	1	10	0	0
1999	CHI	C	107	95	83	560	43	6	8	0	10	42	25	0
1999	CHI	1B	1	0	0	2	0	0	0	0				
2000	CIN	C	84	66	56	428	36	3	4	0	5	19	14	1
2001	SF	C	130	119	107	830	62	5	12	0	8	66	35	0
2001	SF	1B	2	1	0	7	0	0	0	0				
2002	SF	C	125	122	109	738	54	4	10	0	7	58	25	0
2003	SF	C	106	1-6	87	629	34	5	3	0	8	44	10	0
2004	KC	C	49	48	45	228	18	1	3	0	6	28	8	0
2005	PIT	C	6	5	5	43	0	0	0	0	0	3	0	0

Division Series Fielding Record

Year	Team	POS	G	GS	CG	PO	A	ERR	DP	TP	PB	SB	CS	PkO
1995	CIN	C	3	3	3	20	0	0	0	0	0	0	0	0
2002	SF	C	5	5	5	32	2	1	0	0	1	2	1	0
2003	SF	C	11	11	10	69	3	1	1	0	1	4	1	0

League Championship Series Fielding Record

Year	Team	POS	G	GS	CG	PO	A	ERR	DP	TP	PB	SB	CS	PkO
1995	CIN	C	4	4	3	23	1	0	1	0	0	2	1	0
2002	SF	C	5	5	5	24	2	0	1	0	0	1	1	0

World Series Fielding Record

Year	Team	POS	G	GS	CG	PO	A	ERR	DP	TP	PB	SB	CS	PkO
2002	SF	C	7	7	7	40	1	1	0	0	1	6	0	0

*All-Star Game Fielding Record

Year	Team	POS	G	GS	CG	PO	A	ERR	DP	TP	PB	SB	CS	PkO
1989	NL	C	1	1	0	0	0	1	0	0	0	1	0	0
1991	NL	C	1	1	0	4	0	0	0	0	0	0	0	0
1992	NL	C	1	1	0	3	0	0	0	0	0	2	0	0
2002	NL	C	1	0	0	0	0	0	0	0	0	0	0	0

*Selected to 1990 All Star Game and unable to play due to injury prior to game

Author Biographies

Benito Santiago, born in Ponce, Puerto Rico, on March 9, 1965, was in the wave of Latino baseball players who followed in the footsteps of one of his heroes, Roberto Clemente. Raised by Nelida and Modesto Gonzalez in their family after the death of his father, Jose Manuel, Benito knew very little about his birth family until he was ten years old. His early interest in baseball won out over "remaining in the streets," as some of his friends did. In turning to baseball, his talent became especially noticeable in his early teen years. In the common way of the 1980s, a scout set him on the path to enter into the minor league system. Benito signed with the San Diego Padres as a free agent at age seventeen. Designated to be a catcher, he spent four years in the minors, sometimes ready to quit rather than endure the difficulties of low pay and doubt about achieving his dream. In 1986 he was called up to the majors, and in 1987 was named Rookie of the Year for the National League. This was also the year he unveiled what became his legendary ability to throw runners out from his knees. During the career that followed, he played for nine different MLB teams (Cincinnati twice), was selected for five All-Star Games, was on the cover of *Sports Illustrated*, won other awards, and was inducted into the Hispanic Heritage Baseball Museum and Hall of Fame and the San Diego Padres Hall of Fame. He retired in 2005 and is currently involved in different baseball-related activities.

Charlie Hudson, better known for her scuba-themed writing, is a retired U.S. Army officer, who has authored or co-authored numerous novels as well as nonfiction. After her twenty-two-year career that included serving in Desert Shield/Desert Storm and Operation Uphold Democracy in Haiti (1995), she worked as a civilian contractor prior to becoming a full-time freelance writer. All her work can be seen on her website http://charliehudson.net.

Acknowledgments

Benito Santiago

I am so happy to finally have my story told in a book. There are a lot of people in my life to thank and I have talked about many of them in the book. I especially wanted to make sure it was available in Spanish, too.

I want to say an extra thank-you to the players, coaches, managers, sports writers, and ball club staff who are all a part of the great game of baseball. I want to say thank-you to the friends and other family who believed in me before I made it to the majors and who supported me during my career. A very big thank-you goes to the fans. You are why baseball is still such a great sport.

Charlie Hudson

My appreciation, of course, goes to Benito for the time we spent together as he shared memories of both his personal and professional life. It was my friend Sandra (Sandy) Bazinet who proposed the project to me and who worked diligently throughout the process to bring it together.

I am grateful to the individuals cited in the book who provided their insights and memories to give additional dimension to Benito's story.

Marc Appleman of the Society for American Baseball Research (SABR) was of special assistance early in the project as he provided valuable perspective into the world of professional baseball. My thanks also to Charles Gonzalez, who shared his baseball days with me and put me in touch with Mike Rodriguez.

It was Coach James W. Morris III, of the University of Miami, who spoke with me initially about his own love of baseball and his admiration for Benito's skills.

A special thanks to Sherry Roberts, of The Roberts Group, who has once again done a wonderful job of editing.

Fabiola Montanez was great in completing the translation for the Spanish version.

The team at Publish Wholesale expertly brought the book to production, taking it from manuscript to ready for readers.

As always, my husband, Hugh, was with me each step of the way and gave me his loving support.

Notes on Sources

From Charlie Hudson

In reaching back through Benito's memories and contacting selected individuals, the intent of the book was to also provide context of the particular decades in which Benito played. Baseball *is* history, however, and every player who makes it to the big leagues is steeped in the legends of the greats, the ones whose careers were cut short for whatever reason, and the ballparks where thousands of stories have unfolded.

Memories, however, are individual in nature, and people often do not recall any given incident in the same way.

The issue of performance enhancing drugs in baseball and other athletic endeavors has resulted in numerous commissions, investigations, and reports. The memorandum cited in chapter 12, "When Scandal Looms," was issued during the 109th Congress. It was dated March 16, 2005, and sent to Democratic members of the Committee on Government Reform from the Democratic staff in reference to the "Full Committee Hearing on Steroid Use in Baseball." Page two of the seventeen-page memorandum contained the opening paragraph. The memorandum was viewed online September 20, 2016 at https://democratsoversight.house.gov/sites/democrats.oversight.house. gov/files/documents/20050317183306-12546(1).pdf

Special Websites of Interest

1. National Baseball Hall of Fame, http://baseballhall.org/

2. "The History of Latinos in Major League Baseball and Their Growing Influence on the Game" and other segments. A project by Carson Witte and Alex Weick, cited 2017 JAN 8; AC213 Introduction to Latina/o Studies (Gateway redesigned 2004) http://www.umich.edu/~ac213/student_projects06/witaw/index.html

3. The Society for American Baseball Research, http://sabr.org